Unanswered Prayers from "God"

Conversations with the Devil

ASAR ADEWALE FARID

ISBN-13: 978-1-967632-17-6

Printed in the United States of America.

TABLE OF CONTENTS

FOREWORD

This is not a book. It's not fiction. It's not entertainment.

It's a conversation I never thought I'd have. It's a part of me I buried for years — the wounded, wide-eyed boy who cried out to God night after night and got nothing back but silence.

I wrote this because the silence had grown too loud to bear any longer.

I was born into a world that didn't make room for my softness. Where smiles were rare and meals were rationed. Where chickens were fed better than the children who fed them. Where birthdays didn't mean cake — just a few minutes of peace, maybe a piece of meat if we were lucky.

I remember counting peaches on the trees in the summer and praying they'd last us through the winter. I remember being seven and asking God why I had to live like this — why my stomach hurt all the time, why my father's hands knew violence better than love, why I had to borrow sugar from neighbors who looked at me like I was dirt.

And still, I believed. I prayed. I begged Heaven to see me.

I prayed. Hard. I asked God to fix it, to stop it, to take me away. But Heaven never answered. The beatings got worse. The days got longer. And one night, I started imagining something I never thought I'd even consider: killing my father. Not entirely out of hate, but exhaustion. I dreamed about it. Saw it play out in my mind like a movie. I was a child, and already I was rehearsing death.

1

But I didn't do it. I couldn't. Instead, I lived with that guilt too — guilt for what I imagined, and guilt for having survived.

And when God stayed silent, **something else** spoke.

A voice. A presence. One that I called **Shemyaza**. Not holy. Not demonic. Just... *there*. He didn't judge me. He didn't promise salvation. He offered something I hadn't felt in years: understanding. And in my most broken moments — when I was crumpled on the floor with bleach in my lungs, when I was selling crack just to eat, when I was watching a mother offer me her daughter in exchange for a hit — that voice was the only thing that didn't disappear.

I lived enduring physical and mental pain from my father. I helplessly witnessed the assault of my beloved sister. I tried to outrun grief, but it followed me from childhood through every failed promise, every unanswered call, every time I stood in front of a mirror and wondered if I even existed.

I ended up on the side of the highway once, trying to work up the courage to let go, swerve into traffic, and be done with it. But I made one more call. Not to a friend. Not to family. They never answered. I called on the only thing I had left: a sliver of faith.

That call changed everything.

I started therapy. I started healing. I worked jobs no one wanted — chicken plants, warehouses, kitchens where the floor never stopped shaking, and shook my self-esteem like an earthquake.

At school, the kids laughed at my clothes, my smell, and my silence. I wore the same shirt for days. My stomach growled louder than the lessons. They didn't know I hadn't eaten in two days. They mocked us brutally, saying that we lit oil lamps because the electricity had been cut off again. That my siblings and I knocked on doors begging for food while our parents sat inside, too cruel, too broken, to care. My father beat us as if it were a sport. My mother watched, never saying a word. Not once. I'd show up to class with bruises I couldn't explain and shame I didn't have words for. I wasn't just hungry. I was invisible. A kid trying to disappear inside a world that already pretended I wasn't there.

But somehow, through the fear, the trauma, the chaos, I found a thread. A counselor. A stranger who listened. A job that paid just enough. A school with a door left open. And as the tables turned, a Navy recruiter saw something in me that I didn't see in myself. I stood on a stage and got my diploma. No parents in the crowd. Just me. And the voice that never left.

This book isn't wrapped in healing. It's soaked in the blood of becoming.

If you've ever been the kid who sat in the dark and asked why God never came — I know that silence. If you've ever dreamed of escaping pain by becoming someone else, I know that, too.

What you'll read here is not clean. It's not inspirational in the way people like. But it's honest. It's mine. And it might just be yours, too.

If you're ready, walk with me. I'll show you the fire I came through — and how I learned to carry it without burning myself alive.

Let's begin.

—Asar Adewale Farid

Author's Note

"And God said, 'Let there be Light.'"

As I sat in my car on the shoulder of Beltway 495 South, in tears amid the traffic, I realized I had hit rock bottom. I sat there just waiting for the perfect moment – perhaps a speeding tractor-trailer truck would approach so I could pull my vehicle in front of it and end my life. I attempted to call all my friends, but no one answered. I called all my fraternity brothers, and no one answered—all voicemails, no returned calls… just me and my hopelessness. On the shoulder of the 495 South, I sat in that car full of sadness, fear, and lacking the will to survive. I sat there, a broken man. I was no longer the boy who escaped the horrors of physical abuse, but a man who was still within the bondage of emotional and psychological trauma.

That day, I made three more calls that would save and ultimately change the course of my life forever. The first call was a verbal plea to the Creator of the Heavens and Earth. With that plea, I renewed my sense of faith. The second call was to the suicide hotline of Prince George's County. The operator spoke with me for almost an hour and stopped me from driving into that oncoming traffic. That operator also encouraged me to seek the help of a psychologist. She suggested that an ongoing treatment plan was the best thing that I could do, and one of the ways I could escape the pain that I felt.

This novel is a result of my renewed faith in the Creator and a corresponding hope for humanity. Because of my attending therapy, psychological treatment, and all the prayers and support from my siblings, I got better. The words written within the confines of these pages are a representation of all the years of uncertainty, paranoia, and all the tears that I couldn't cry. This book's existence is predicated on all the sadness and fear behind my happy faces and smiles. This is a living, breathing testimony of all the pain, tears, terror, abandonment, and sadness I felt as a child. Ultimately, this book exists as my call to action for all the millions and millions of little boys and girls who are living through abuse every single day. All those children who are suffering great, unbearable pain inflicted by those whom they trust.

Who is willing to be that beacon of light, that beacon of hope, and will stand to protect our children? Who will have the courage to fight for those children who cannot stand up for themselves? Who is willing to break that darkness of silence and give light to the voiceless? Who will free our children from bondage?

Facts: National Statistics on Child Abuse

In 2015, an estimated 1,670 children died from abuse and neglect in the United States. In 2015, Children's Advocacy Centers around the country served more than 311,000 child victims of abuse, providing victim advocacy and support to these children and their families.

Nearly 700,000 children are abused in the U.S annually. An estimated 683,000 children (unique incidents) were victims of abuse and neglect in 2015, the most recent year for which there is national data.

CPS protects more than 3 million children. Approximately 3.4 million children received an investigation or alternative response from child protective services agencies. 2.3 million children received prevention services.

The youngest children were most vulnerable to maltreatment. Children in the first year of their life had the highest rate of victimization of 24.2 per 1,000 children in the national population of the same age.

Neglect is the most common form of maltreatment. Of the children who experienced maltreatment or abuse, three-quarters suffered neglect; 17.2% suffered physical abuse; and 8.4% suffered sexual abuse. (Some children are poly-victimized—they have suffered more than one form of maltreatment.) About four out of five abusers are the victims' parents. A parent of the child victim was the perpetrator in 78.1% of substantiated cases of child maltreatment.

"Childhood sexual abuse is a topic that desperately needs attention in the African-American community, yet not enough people talk about it above a whisper."

Stefanie Hargrove

American Psychological Association, 2014

Chapter One

Genesis

Our Father in heaven, hallowed be your name. Your Kingdom come, your will be done, on Earth as in heaven. Give us today our daily bread. Forgive us for our sins, as we forgive those who sin against us. Lead us not into temptation, but deliver us from evil. For the kingdom, the power, and the glory are yours now and forever.

Amen.

Why? Per Webster's dictionary, 'Why' is the common word used to define the meaning of reason, or for what purpose. This simple yet powerful word has been the starting point of many historical events throughout recorded human history. For me, it has been the spark to explore a fiery conquest throughout my own life. In my quest for enlightenment, I have sought to understand 'why' and the processes and interplay of my personal experiences.

As the roads lead me to ascertain many answers, they have also made me realize there are twice as many questions. Why am I here at this particular moment in my life? Why have all these pitfalls and hills happened to me? Why doesn't God answer my prayers or even talk to me? Why have His blessings, protection, teachings, and many esoteric connotations eluded me all these years? Why? I ask, why? This one question, this singular word which contains so much power, is and will continue to be the endless flame of my journey.

How did I arrive here at this moment? According to many faiths that many men follow, it is God's destiny. To many, it is the will of God that allows me to exist in this very moment. Is it the grand

7

design of the Great Architect of the Universe in which my thoughts are conceived and actions carried out? I do not have the definite answers to these questions, nor will I ever during this lifetime. I believe I will only acquire these answers and secrets to life when I transition to the next realm of existence and gain a deeper understanding of it.

Although I ask these lifelong questions, I appreciate where I am today. I've come to deeply understand how my past has shaped my thoughts, feelings, and approach to navigating the world. Every experience has left its mark — molding my thoughts, guiding my actions, and carving deep channels through my emotions. My sense of self, my view of family, the world around me, and all the souls within it have been deeply and irrevocably affected by what I call my past.

The past — a time that, for me, has been filled mostly with pain, heartache, and abandonment. It leaves a trail of emotional emptiness, confusion, loneliness, and a lingering lack of clarity. Why have I earned these lashes of despair and hopelessness across my back? What did I do to deserve these misunderstood blessings? As I look above to the starry-filled Canopy, the Heavens above, with just that one question. Why? Answer me, please, God.

* * * * *

On a crisp and serene spring morning, on Monday, May 5th, to be exact, the "Phoenix" rose from Her ashes yet again. As above in the Heavens, there existed not a cloud in that pre-dawn sky. On that glorious morning, the Moon sat peacefully upon Her throne as Her many constellations draped Her in illumination with the utmost arrogance. At one precise moment of 3:33, the Great Architect of the Universe gave me to my mother and father. As my consciousness came into existence in a physical form, the path of my destiny began as a living, breathing entity in this world, as I understood it.

My earliest memories date back to when I was 5 years old. At that time, my family was living in Abbeville, Alabama. The only other siblings at that time were my oldest sister, Dawn, who is five years my senior, and my younger brother, Jim, who is two years my junior. Most of my recollection involves Dawn and me at home by ourselves. My mother and father were not home often. That, of course, was a different story once the weekends came. Even then, it was my sister babysitting me while they were out and about. Dawn taught me my ABCs and numbers from 1 to 20, forwards and backwards. I even credit my older sister for teaching me to pick up behind myself and how to complete small household chores. I suppose she could have foreshadowed that these skills would be necessary for my success and independence.

Dawn was so energetic in those days. She loved to laugh, was very playful, and was a highly skilled dancer. We would play for hours in the yard; she would push me on my bike and in my space shuttle wagon. Those were the days of long ago. The days of sunshine and peace before the storm came upon our shores of existence. Our peace lasted for almost two years before the other five siblings came. My other brothers and sisters were a complete blessing to us without question, but to my parents, we became a virus, a foreign entity that they wished to rid themselves of.

I recall often asking myself, 'What is happiness?' Happiness to me in those days was the laughs and cries I shared with the seven of us. Nothing could replace that, not by a long shot. As I reached the age of 7, watching the other kids in the neighborhood do things we couldn't do, I never understood why kids the same age as me wouldn't be home during the summer, while I sat at home. Kids would talk about their trips to the beach and the pool, and I had nothing to tell them. No beach, no parks, no smiles and laughs to share with the other kids.

I sat at home those early summers, feeding our chickens and goats in the humid Alabama heat. I should be having fun too, I thought to myself. Why not us? By the time I started 1st grade, kids would tell their summer camp stories to the class about how they went on vacation. From my point of view, their vacations were never extravagant; at least, I thought they weren't. However, they spent quality time together as a family. I wanted that too. I wanted to play with my dad, throwing the football. I wanted to play with my brother in the sand and fish with my mom, just like all the other kids.

I believe that a child's early years in life should be enriched with exposure to a wide range of experiences. It should be a period of enlightenment and openness to the universal energies of growth. As a child grows, they should begin to establish their identity and self-awareness, developing an understanding of their existence in the reality we call life. My physical frame was somewhat stunted in its growth process due to the lack of proper nourishment. As a boy, I was always smaller than the other kids. Most of my peers experienced their growth spurts around the age of 13, but mine was delayed by almost five years.

As my years progressed, my childhood experience became destructive and cold, to no fault of my own. If I could describe the pains and agony of my childhood experiences, it could be summarized in one word: hunger.

My six other siblings and I suffered from hunger most of our early years. We starved for nourishment in every aspect. Nourishment that is essential to a child's growth from many perspectives. The perspective of hunger we experienced clouded our views of our world. Fighting the pains of an aching belly, a cold heart, and an empty mind. The pursuit to eliminate hunger pangs was the driving force, the quintessential foundation of our survival.

For us, there was very little food. Most of the time, our meals included beans, greens, and some form of bread. My "Father" and "Mother " regulated the meat in our household." How fucking selfish of them to keep all the meat for themselves.

As a child, one of the many animals that our parents bought was chickens. Chickens that required a lot of attention. The chickens needed fresh straw to lay their eggs, a weekly change of water to drink, and chicken feed so they could eat. My siblings and I were primarily responsible for the daily maintenance and upkeep of these chickens. Those stinky, loud, shitty, nasty ass chickens really got on my last nerve. All around the perimeter of our home, they would roam and scratch up the grass and shrubs. Those chickens often got into the blueberry and strawberry patches, causing absolute havoc and chaos. But in the end, it was those very chickens that would help change the course of my future.

When the chores around the house, especially tending to the chickens, were neglected, the beatings were brutal. Really fucking brutal. How dare we have the audacity to forget to feed the chickens or dust the windows! All the effort we put into the upkeep of the chickens and that house, we rarely had a chance to experience the fruits of our labor. The taste of fried, baked, and barbecued chicken was reserved for the ruthless, heartless dictators who ruled our home—unless it was a special day, one of our birthdays or holidays.

There was minimal food for the seven of us. Most of my childhood days were spent starving. In fact, the best and most filling times of the year were spring and summer. During those months, we had a plethora of fruit trees surrounding our house that produced many tasty snacks. I'm talking about peaches, apples, plums, as well as strawberries and blueberries, which were all within our grasp. Along with the fruit, we also had several vegetable gardens that gave us high quantities of greens, squash, and potatoes. When those hunger pains often came, we would go to the fruit trees and partake in their sweet offerings. In those good old days, the Sun and its warmth and light proved to be our Savior. We knew if God's Sun was resurrected every day, we wouldn't starve. Our praises were strong during the Spring and Summer as the fruits of Our God filled our shallow bellies. To save some of our fruits and vegetables for later use, we would attempt to freeze some of the food for the winter months. This didn't work well due to our limited knowledge of canning and food preservation. We were too young to replicate the skills of grandmothers who were masters of the craft.

When those frosty, numbing winters came, we longed for the food we had in the Spring and Summer. Those sneaky, cold Alabama winters proved to be the worst times for us. No fruits, no vegetables, no meat, no love, no joy, just US. We mostly survived on the frozen beans and peas we got from our grandmothers and homemade bread. Sometimes, the hunger pains would be so severe that it would lead us to fight amongst ourselves.

Not for lack of love for one another, but the increased frustration caused by the void of food led to our dissension. Those hunger pains led to mental frustrations, and those mental frustrations were transmogrified to the rumblings that echoed in our bellies like the violent strikes of lightning and thunder of a summer storm. Consequently, those violent rumblings turned us against one another. We fought like we were possessed by demons—demons who had been set out to feast upon our fears of death.

The Demons, who somehow could read and preoccupy our thoughts, somehow knew we had no faith in our parents and that we feared tasting death by starving. They preoccupied our judgments— brother versus brother, sister versus sister—as if all for the entertainment and pleasure of the people who gave us life.

Why? I would ask.

Why wouldn't they give us nourishment we so needed and desired? Why would they turn their back upon our helpless faces? We didn't ask to be here in this world! Why would they neglect the living, breathing seeds He planted?

Why would He not intervene and rescue His most incredible creation from turmoil and despair? These pains of hope and despair were the earliest basis of my prayers to God:

God, please help us! I NEED YOU SO MUCH!!!

CHAPTER TWO

So Many Questions

Bismillaah ar-Rahman ar-Raheem Al hamdu lillaahi rabbil 'alameen ArRahman ar-Raheem Maaliki yaumid Deen Iyyaaka na'abudu wa iyyaaka nasta'een Ihdinas siraatal mustaqeem Siraatal ladheena an 'amta' alaihim Ghairil maghduubi' alaihim waladaaleen

Aameen.

In the name of God, the infinitely Compassionate and Merciful. Praise be to God, Lord of all the worlds, the Compassionate, the Merciful Ruler on the Day of Reckoning. You alone do we worship, and You alone do we ask for help. Guide us on the straight path, the path of those who have received your grace; not the path of those who have brought down wrath, nor of those who wander astray.

Amen.

I often wondered why my parents had so many children when they either refused or simply couldn't take care of us. There were constant arguments between them, both verbal and physical. Most often, the fights were about money or something tied to it. One argument I remember vividly was over who was supposed to fill out the paperwork for food stamps. The deadline was approaching quickly, and neither of them wanted to go into town to get it done. I sat on the edge of my bed and listened. The walls in my room were paper thin, so every word came through as if they were shouting right in front of me.

They continued to fuss and cuss, each attempting to justify why the other was obligated to complete the task. I was bold enough to knock on the door while that fussed. "What the fuck you want?!" he yelled. I didn't respond at all because fear coursed through my veins. Silence was behind the door all at once. I was hesitant, but I knocked on the door again. I stood in fear as I heard the footsteps quicken at the door. I opened with a rush of air as the door swung open with a certain virtuosity. There he stood, his facial expression told of the agreement that ensued behind the door.

"What?!"

I shuddered a bit, but gathered my thoughts collectively. I then ask, "What's for dinner? I'm hungry." My stomach growled as he stared at me.

"Drink some water, that will fill you up." The argument ended with them both saying, "I guess they're not going to eat." Neither budged that day. For dinner, we had cheese sandwiches and fried potatoes that my sister, Dawn, had fixed for us.

I later found out that the paperwork was never filled out. For two months, our grandmothers fed all seven of us with what they could muster from their fixed incomes. Not only did we lack food, but we also lacked the proper nourishment for our hearts and minds. As growing children, we didn't experience much love at all. In fact, I can count on one hand the number of times my parents showed that they somewhat cared about our well-being. Those unknown, unspoken words that mean so much to all children, all adults, all human beings, somehow escaped the tongue of my parents. Never did those precious words flow from their lips. That void that all children have, that is left to be filled by their Creators, remained empty. Only the sands of time would eventually fill my heart with that essence, a feeling and sense of worthiness, Love of myself.

I was always confused how mother and father looked themselves in the mirror, knowing what they were doing to us. They were both college-educated, and for the most part, their education was paid for by their parents. Why wasn't the same opportunity afforded to us as well? Why not a better life for us? Why? My father graduated from Tuskegee Institute, and my mother graduated from nursing school. The ability and means to enamor us with wisdom and knowledge were there, but somehow, they couldn't pass on to us what was needed to lay a foundation of success.

My father also couldn't keep a consistent job. I remember him continually saying, "The White man is trying to hold me back." As a child, I didn't know any better, so I took him at his word to be true. Maybe the White man was trying to keep an educated black man from rising and becoming a shining success. It was highly possible, I mean we did grow up in racist ass Alabama during the late 70's; but in the back of my mind I would often ask, if it is so hard here, why not move? We had family in Georgia, Florida, and other parts of the country. What is keeping us here? Why do we continue to be hungry here if there are other places that can be better?

We had encyclopedia sets in the house, and I would always look at other states in the U.S. What if we could move to Texas or even North Carolina? What would life be like in California? Oh, hell yes! The beach all year round, shit let's go! That sounded fun, but too good to be true. Alabama was our personal Hell – no way out unless Death, itself, carried me to the pearly gates to which I had been promised.

How was it possible that two college-educated people, my parents, struggled to put food on the table? In comparison to the other families in my city, most parents had barely completed high school. But here we were, both parents with college degrees, and we had to borrow sugar and food from the neighbors. I suppose they were too embarrassed to do it themselves, but they would always send us to do their dirty work. My sister and I would sometimes have to ask our neighbors to borrow food so we could eat. I hated that shit, but it never failed. At the end of the month, especially if we were unable to submit the food stamp paperwork on time, Dawn and I had to beg for food. Bread, sugar, and cheese were the easiest things to get. Rarely did we get meat; even though pork was the cheapest option at the time, we weren't allowed to eat pork.

Borrowing food made us easy targets for bullies, as we were constantly the subject of gossip. As soon as we arrived at school, people would know about our having to borrow food, and then the questions and jokes smothered us like the stifling heat of those humid Alabama summers.

Why don't y'all have food? Y'all ain't got no money? I heard your daddy ain't working? Why y'all stay in that raggedy ass house? I heard y'all water off, is that true? Y'all ain't pay the utility bills?

It was horrible! It seemed they knew everything that was going on at my house. All of our secrets became the town talk. How did they know we used 5-gallon buckets for the bathroom, since my home had no running water? How did they know we used oil lamps and the fireplace, since we had no money for the electricity bill? It was too much for a kid to handle sometimes… many a day, I would run out of class to the bathroom and cry my heart out. While shedding tears, my head would look to the sky in prayer. Please make it stop, God Almighty. Please! Make it stop! No answer from Heaven above, just more jokes that lead to more tears. The more people talked and joked about us, the more I looked to my father for guidance and reassurance. I wanted to know that it would be alright, and these struggles would only last for a short time. But he, too, as did God, turned his back upon my cries.

My father and I had an emotionless relationship. There was no bond, no sense of worthiness, nor any compassion. I longed for his love and approval. What more does a son desire than to have his father exclaim, "I'm so proud of you, son!" What more does a son ask of his father but unconditional love?

What can be more pleasing to a young man's ears than to hear those sweet words, "Son, I am the proudest dad in the world!" I heard nothing from him. I was the saddest little boy in the whole world. I felt so very empty, yet I was full of all those unwanted emotions. As a little boy, I so badly wanted to run to my dad and hug him, have him tell me he loved me, but from him, I got nothing but coldness. I starved for his love, his companionship, his approval. Nothingness, emptiness, and uncertainty filled my heart and mind in those days. Dear God, why does my father forsake me? Why Lord? Why won't you talk to me?

CHAPTER THREE

Hunger Pains

Dear God,

Please help me! Please! I pray to you every night and hope you hear me, but I'm not sure if you do or not. Why won't you answer me? Was I disobedient to you, too? Today I got in trouble for something I didn't do. Can you talk to my daddy for me? Tell him to stop hurting me, please. Especially when he puts my head in the tub full of water, it makes me black out. Dear God, please! I don't know if I'm a good son or not, but I want to make my daddy proud! I don't think he loves me either. Can't you please talk to me? I feel like I'm going to die, can you not let me die?

Amen.

As the hunger pangs of my life grew to an unbearable apex, there came an unexpected relief. The rumblings and growlings inside my stomach were quickly satisfied and replaced by a different set of pains. The nourishment I received was not from the variety of food, but from the results of beatings. The beatings caused pains that were so great, so much more intense, that I completely forgot about the need for food and love. By the age of six, I was subject to "beatings" from my mother and father every week. I never understood why all the anger and hatred suddenly entered my life, but there they appeared. The beatings were a force of nature that would change the outlook and course of my life forever.

Looking back at that period of my life, I can say with near certainty that three things felt almost guaranteed. First, there was an inevitable loneliness and absence in my heart. My parents never spent a lot of time at home. My siblings and I found solace within ourselves and in each other. For the most part, there was little family time at home. I would always wish for movie nights or simply just time, just to talk and bond. In the absence of love, we spent most of the intimate moments with each other.

Secondly, my sister persevered as the protector for me and the rest of us. Dawn had our backs all the time. She was guarding the kingdom just as the flaming sword protected the Tree of Everlasting Life that God banished from Eden.

The third harsh reality in my life at that time was the beatings — brutal ones, at least three times a week. For no good reason at all, I was beaten and assaulted with great malice and ill intent. My ass whoopings were so fierce and intense, I could feel the hatred from his hands with every strike. During the Transatlantic Slave Trade, the efforts of enslavers were to subdue the will of fresh enslaved Africans by tremendous beatings and floggings in public; these same strategies of psychological and mental submission took place in my home.

These floggings always happened in front of my other brothers and sisters. I can say they witnessed every beating I got and vice versa. It was always open for all to see. My mother would even watch. Sometimes I would even call her name in helpless abandonment, but to no avail. Most times, she would turn the other cheek as the continuous strikes tore skin from my legs, arms, and back. From my mouth, I yelled for my mother, but in my mind, I sought a higher power. After the beatings, I would lie gingerly in my bed, with ice on the bruises that I could reach, and I would pray to God. Most of the time, my prayers were for the pain to go away that I had received. At other times, it was to make the beatings stop. God never answered. In fact, by the age of 9, the beatings only got far worse.

Oftentimes, Dawn would come in to console me after I would curl up in a pool of my tears. We knew we needed each other, and she was there just as I was for her. "It will be ok, little brother, I got one too." Her efforts were always met with my smile as she told me, "This too shall pass." It seemed as if my mother would punish her far worse than my dad beat me. My mother would be so angry that she would lock my sister in the closet for the weekend. Her time in the dark closet would start on Saturday mornings and end on Sunday evenings. She wasn't even allowed to drink water or eat food. Only darkness, pain, and hatred were what she received from the people who were supposed to give us LOVE. I would sit on the floor next to her and talk to her to see how she was doing. There wasn't much I could do because the closet used to be locked from the outside, and my mother had the key.

On Sunday afternoons, she was allowed out. When she would exit the closet, it would be covered and filled with my sister's feces and urine. She could only sit there in that tiny, dark space and ponder her existence. Just as the enslaved people on the first ships crossed the Atlantic, she sat there. No nourishment, just pissing and shitting on herself in complete darkness. Countless times, Dawn endured these lave-like punishments and treatments. I always believed that we were intentionally made to feel less than human. We were subjected to indescribable pain that was inflicted upon us as my parents mimicked the slave masters of days gone past. It often felt like they were angry at us simply for existing, as if our very presence was a burden they never asked for. But we didn't choose to be here. We never asked for this life.

To be treated as though we were unloved and unwanted was deeply demoralizing.

My father used various weapons when it came to beating me. I believe his optimal selection of a punishment tool was anything he put his hands on at that moment. Still, his top three were an electric extension cord, a 2x4 that came from a failed remodeling project, and a wooden broom handle. I often wondered how a man who stood only 5'6' and 170 pounds could be full of so much anger and hate. How could a man of that stature inflict so much punishment?

Anything that he thought would inflict as much pain as possible, he would use it. Why? We weren't bad kids. We made decent grades. What made my parents seem to hate us? Maybe they didn't want us, or perhaps they didn't wish to each other? Regardless, we felt the pain and wrath of their poor decisions and insecurities. All the beatings were easy in comparison to my father's choices of punishment. A punishment I greatly feared more so than any tree branch or extension cord. A punishment that left a deep-rooted fear in the recesses of my mind. As ominous as he was to me, his preferred means of demoralizing me was the Water.

CHAPTER FOUR

The Trash Man Cometh

God, please hear my prayer. Can you help me, please? What do you want me to do? Do you hear me? Why won't you answer me? I know I can be a better son, but I prayed to you five times today, and you still won't talk back? He keeps hitting me and my sister hard. I can't sleep on my back; it hurts so bad. It seems like my mother and he fight all the time. Why did you let her just watch us get beaten? I'm having trouble with my asthma, too, and we can't go to the doctor. It's hard to even talk to you now. Can you help me? Please?

Amen.

As a young man, I was often assigned a long list of household chores, a common experience for most boys growing up in the South at that time. These tasks were meant to teach me responsibility and accountability, values I'd one day be expected to carry into my household. Of course, these lessons weren't explained to me by my father, but rather by my uncles and other older male figures I encountered throughout my upbringing.

One of my primary responsibilities as the oldest boy in the house was taking out the trash regularly. In our neighborhood, the trash man only came once a week — and with a family of nine, you can imagine how much garbage piled up over seven days. It was a lot. The main trash can was always filled to the brim, with at least three extra bags stacked beside the overflowing thirteen-gallon bin.

The challenge wasn't just the volume but ensuring it all arrived on time. The trash man would come like clockwork between 6:30 and 7:30 every Thursday morning, unless it were a holiday. For me, that meant it was absolutely crucial to take the trash out the night before. If I overslept, I risked missing him — and with that much trash, missing pickup was not an option.

One normal evening, as I prepared to take the trash out to the street, as I always did in anticipation of the trash truck's arrival, I heard a voice within me. That evening, a voice so subtle guided me to put the trash further up the driveway than usual. I placed the trash can right next to the stand-alone mail box. At this point, I wasn't sure why I was having this notion, but I did. My driveway was a little different from the other homes in my neighborhood. Our driveway was a combination of clay and dirt, extending almost 20 yards from the front door of the house to the edge of the street. Nonetheless, it was a tough walk while simultaneously rolling about 40 pounds of trash.

As I took heed to that whisper that night, I placed the trash just slightly further up than usual. Later that night, a thunderstorm entered the area. This thunderstorm brought with it high winds and heavy rains. I came out the next morning and witnessed that most of our neighbors' trash had been blown over, and it was strewn all over the road and the yards of other neighbors. Miraculously, our trash can had fallen over only to be supported by the mailbox that stood beside it. As the winds blew, so did all the trash across the grass. Just as I got on the bus, the trash man picked up the can and dumped it on his truck. At that point, I was greatly relieved, knowing that I had made yet another deadline and I wouldn't be in trouble.

Later that day, I got off the bus and saw my father's car in the yard, which was a little odd because he rarely was home when I got out of school. At that moment, the voice returned, just as it had suddenly appeared in my thoughts the previous night. Don't go in that house, it whispered. I was startled, frightened by the sound of the voice. It was as clear as if another person were standing beside me. I ignored that warning, although I had not the previous evening. Walking down my driveway slowly gave me time to gather my thoughts and interact with my father. As I drew closer to the door, I felt the familiar gurgle in my stomach, the increase in my heart rate, and the heaviness in my lungs, all signs that I had experienced many times before.

Fear.

As I entered my house, I slowly opened the door. Before stepping in, I took one last deep breath before facing my fears. "What I tell you about taking the trash out!" he yelled.

"I did take it out, I just pulled the trash can in further." At this point, I'm trembling severely, as I am anticipating getting badly beaten.

"So why all that fucking trash out there?" I couldn't respond. I was in complete shock. Frozen in fear, now only God can save me from the inevitable. "Bring your ass in this bathroom!"

I nervously walked towards the bathroom, already in tears, awaiting my fate. God please! God please! You know, I took out the trash. Let him have mercy on me today, please, God, please! Yet as before, God didn't respond to me in my time of peril.

I entered the bathroom, and there it was, my reckoning. By this time, the tub was filled halfway with cold water. A roll of three towels was neatly folded next to the tub. He grabbed me by the arm harshly and shoved me to the floor with vicious intent. "Put your knees on the towel! How many times do I have to tell you to take out that trash? This is gonna help you remember!" My father grabbed my neck forcibly and submerged my head under the cold water. Ten seconds later, my head was raised back up.

I gasped for precious breaths. He yelled and cursed loudly, but I couldn't hear him completely because of the waterlogged in my ears. After the second or third attempt, I caught my breath. I yelled, "I'm sorry, Father, I'm sorry!" Although in my mind I knew I did nothing wrong, and it was the neighbor's trash that was about our yard, there was no mercy for me as my head was taken underneath the water for a second and third time with his grip.

My body squirmed and fought against the water entering my mouth and nose. I lost count of how many times my head met that bathtub that day, but I woke up 10 minutes later feeling completely drained of all my energy. The taste of the water still rippled bitterly against my taste buds. As I gained more consciousness, I now realized that the very water that my head was dunked in, which caused my world to go temporarily dark, contained Clorox bleach. Now my eyes burned feverishly from the contaminants that they were exposed to. The clothes I had on from head to toe were soaked. I lay there on that cold bathroom floor, wondering why this had happened. Why didn't God help me when I begged for His mercy? My God, why had you forsaken me? My father tried to kill me, I thought to myself. My somber thoughts then became uncontrollable tears, knowing that he just left me there on that cold floor, unconscious. I sobbed for almost another fifteen minutes as I lay in the fetal position. I felt there was no hope in sight, only despair.

Was this going to be my fate – a destiny of heartache and agony? How long can I live with this burden of fear and pain? Why doesn't my father love me like all the other fathers love their sons? Why doesn't my "Father" hear and answer my calls? I now know that through his actions, he showed me that I was just a fuck up, an unwanted kid to him. I'm just a disappointment to him and my mother. Why not just let me live with my grandmother or another family? I just have to ensure that all the trash in the yard is picked up so that he won't think it's our trash. I hate that fucking bathtub, but I hate that mutha fucking trash man even more!

CHAPTER FIVE

God's Infinite Silence

God, please hear me! Why won't you talk to me? We need help here in this house, your precious temple. There is no love over here. I make salat, and I say my prayers regularly. I do what your Quran instructs me to do! Please forgive me for my sins; I need you to hear me! Hear me, please! It's hard to live anymore. Please answer me to let me know you are there. God please. Let me know if I will be okay. Please!

Amen.

The day after, I woke up on that cold, wet floor; I had a different feeling about myself. I couldn't explain it, but the feeling of change was there. Inside me was a distinct sensation I had never experienced before in my life. The voice that guided me to place the trash can against the mailbox and not go inside the house now had a different meaning. I initially thought I had gotten into trouble because of the trash. After further contemplation, I then reckoned that there was no misunderstanding. My father would beat me whether the garbage was in the can or sprawled across the lawn. The trash strewn about the yard was just an excuse to inflict his torture and relieve the stress of his failures.

After that, I felt like I had changed for the worse. Unlike the Phoenix and its scorching grave, I had to rise from a watery death that was supposed to be my undoing. The fear of drowning was engraved in the very fabric of my consciousness. I became less joyful and playful than I was before the incident. I was more defensive and protective of my words and actions. I walked ever so cautiously, constantly aware of my steps, making sure not to break the eggshell that was my father's temper. I learned to keep my eyes open in the shower, even while washing my hair. The sting of the shampoo in my eyes was no comparison to the flashbacks of ice water in my lungs. The images of that painful day would constantly reappear over and over, wreaking havoc on the synapses of my mind. That feeling of drowning and hopelessness haunted my thoughts and dreams daily.

Months passed, and I still didn't know what to make of the foreign voice that spoke to me. Maybe it was God talking to me after all this time.

Maybe He is finally answering my prayers... Prayers that I have offered for several years, but never reached Him in the deep, distant silence. Why now, if it is Him, that has come to fulfill my desperate request? Is it Him now that cometh to reinstate hope in my heart, mind, and soul?

My conclusions left me empty and uneasy. The more I tried to figure out what or who this voice was, the more confused I became. The more I pondered, the less fulfilled I became with the conclusion of my wonderings. Did this voice that I hear carry the mighty words of God? Were the words ringing in my eardrums part of my vivid imagination? If I asked my mother, she would think I'm crazy. Hell, anyone would think a kid who heard voices is crazy. All my questions led me to answers that left me increasingly feeling hopeless and empty. Deep down in my heart, I knew the answers to the questions I sought.

One night, just before I closed my eyes to sleep, the voice called my name. It was very subtle and clear yet demanding and powerful— so vivid, as if the source was right beside my bed. I was fearful. As I pulled the covers over my head in terror, the voice kept calling my name with specific intent: "Wale...

Wale…"

I didn't respond; I was too afraid. I wanted to respond badly, but I held back my words. In fear, I recited Surah Al-Nasr, which I had learned from the mosque. This surah is performed in times of need for protection from an evil presence. At that moment of saying amen, the voice abruptly stopped calling my name. I dozed off that night in peace, but I still wondered if the source of the voice was in my head or if there was someone I couldn't see.

Two nights had passed without any further incidents of me hearing that demanding voice. On that third evening, I lay on my bed and closed my eyes. I gently inhaled and exhaled as my body became acclimated to the hard mattress I slept on every night. I shut my eyes and thought about what school would be like the following day. I wondered about completing all my homework, and I was very excited about the upcoming field trip on Friday. Finally, after one last deep breath, I closed my eyes. "Wale!" the voice exclaimed.

I lay there in silence. This time, I was not as fearful as I was before. "Mr. Farid, I know you hear me," the voice said softly. With all my might, I wished this voice would stop speaking to me, but there was no end to this night; I had to answer him.

"Yes?" I replied. There was a pregnant pause as I breathed deeply in anticipation, awaiting the voice to speak back.

"You will fear no more, my son, no more pain. I am here to guide and help you. Do you understand?" the voice said. I slowly whispered yes from my lips as my heart raced at this unique moment, this awkward conversation. I gathered the courage to pull back the covers from my face, only to see nothing but my brother in his bed. I whispered his name, but he lay there quietly in deep sleep. At that moment, I knew that it wasn't him playing games, and that the voice was real.

"Mr. Wale," the voice spoke. "I am with you from this moment forward. Do you understand?"

I paused to breathe and slowly answered, "Yes."

The next words that came from my mouth that humid evening would change my life forever. The answers that I sought would be answered in a matter of seconds. The fulfillment that I wanted was about to fill my soul with undeniable reassurance. This evening, all the prayers offered to God were met with a mystical response. The voice continued to speak to me, but I couldn't focus on His words because questions ran through my head.

Without any prompt, I questioned the voice with bravery and zeal. "Are you God here to answer my prayers?!" There was no response, and the voice was dreadfully silent. "Are you the 'Devil'?!" I heard a slight chuckle, almost like a confirmation or an admission of guilt.

The voice then whispered with comfort and reassurance, "I am what you require, regardless of what you call me. I am your redeemer. I am not God, but your savior. I am all that you want, your beacon of light. I am the answer to your prayers. He heard you, too, but chose not to respond. I heard you as well, and here I am. I am your SAVIOR!" Though there was uncertainty in my thoughts, I believed him. "Will you accept me?" he asks. "Will you put your faith in me?"

Without hesitation or reservation, I answered, "Yes!"

CHAPTER SIX

The Fire Rises

God,

If you can hear me, please answer. I feel like I'm going to die. I think my father wants me dead. He watches me as if he's studying or plotting to kill me. Please help me! Thoughts of death are in my mind consistently. I don't want to die, so here I am asking for your mercy. I still want to believe in you, but I need your guidance. In your name, I pray.

Amen.

As I accepted the new Savior in my life, there was a resurgence of energy through my body and mind. Now, at age eleven, I was having full-fledged conversations with the "Devil." This "Devil" provided me comfort and solace from all the pain I endured in my house and life. Sometimes, we would talk while I was conscious, but he mostly spoke to me in my dreams. He provided me with a sense of confidence, hope, pleasure, and, more importantly, peace of mind.

Whenever I felt the stress of everyday life or pain from the beatings I received, he was there. This "Devil" was like clockwork, no questions asked, and always on time. He only required me to have faith and trust in him. The "Devil" took me in his bosom and gave me the strength I needed to stay alive. So many days I wished I wouldn't have to live anymore, but he always showed up when I was in despair. He gave me the fight, the will, the need to want to live. Every night, he would whisper "I love you," as if he were my earthly father. He filled the void that my parents created from their abuse.

My own personal "Devil" taught me not only how to shelter my feelings and emotions, but how to survive. I often wondered what if the stories in the Bible, the Quran, and the Torah were wrong. What if it was God who was jealous and hateful, and who left his most incredible creation on their own in the wilderness that we called life? Maybe the stories of Lucifer, Set, and Prometheus were right, and they were cast out of Heaven for their love of humankind. Maybe these angelic beings brought true illumination and wisdom to humans, thus raising them from their shallow graves of ignorance.

God taught man in His Ten Commandments that children should

honor thy mother and honor thy father. Why didn't my mother and father honor me as a blessing from the Creator of the Heavens and Universe, and treat me as such? Isn't that the point? For a child to learn to honor their parent, they must be taught how to do so. A parent should teach their children to cherish and respect themselves, other human beings, and, of course, their parents.

Is there a God? This very question would go through my mind constantly on many lonely and painful nights. God or no God, I couldn't answer that question at that time. All I knew were the beatings that continued to be inflicted upon my flesh and mind consistently. As the beatings continued, so did my disdain for what we call God. My anger and pain grew immensely. My anger then grew into vicious hatred.

Soon, I believe that this hatred manifested into health restrictions. I couldn't rely on my body due to the increase in asthma attacks I experienced. The days became shorter due to the inability to play outside with the other children. Playing outside was a minor distraction from what awaited me at home. I could hardly remember doing the things that used to make me smile anymore. Riding my bike, playing tackle football, or even shooting hoops in my cousin's backyard were now an afterthought. The asthma stripped me of what made me smile – it took what I called happiness away as it constricted my lungs.

The lack of oxygen made me look more inward. I became more self-reflective and withdrawn. I even felt the need to avoid my parents. While I stayed back home mostly and withdrew from the physical activities, I started to observe my sister Dawn doing housework and all the small things that keep a household together. She was also the best at cooking. She would usually cook more than my mother and father combined. Dawn was like an American honeybee, small in stature, but a relentless worker. She was only 5'5 in height, weighing only about 130 pounds, but she worked feverishly in and out of our home. Every time she cooked, I asked questions about how to get food to taste and look a certain way. After a while, I eventually decided to try my hand at the craft of cooking. The more I attempted to cook, the quicker I realized how much I thoroughly enjoyed the art of cooking.

In fact, I enjoyed it to the point where it was almost therapeutic; cooking took my mind to places I only envisioned going. I even took up reading Julia Child's cookbooks, which my mother had lying around the house. Julia Child also had a TV show that came on PBS. Julia was so charismatic and joyful when she cooked. She sometimes had her guests over to try some of her finished products, which she had been cooking for the day.

Like the sun rises every day, her guests always smile and laugh blissfully at the taste of her freshly prepared food. I wanted to smile and experience the same happiness as her guests always did. My sister's cooking made me smile and brought joy to all of us. At times, I was so thankful for the set of faulty asthmatic lungs that lay within my rib cage. Those asthmatic lungs allowed me to watch pure joy and craftsmanship through Julie Child.

Aside from attempting to cook, and studying my sister's movements, reading – another hobby – became like breathing to me. As I read, I envisioned the words jumping off the page, performing a concert for my eyes only. Reading books allowed me to travel to places beyond my small, dusty, deprived town in Alabama. Reading was part of my escape from the horrors of my reality. On days after it stopped raining in the morning, I would grab a blanket and escape to the woods behind my house. The woods always provided me the perfect solace; once I went beyond the thickness of the bushes, there lay a beautiful clearing of green grass seemingly just for me. The clearing almost resembled the shape of a triangle or square. I, then, could really dive into my books and escape the horrors of my house.

The cool morning rains would wash away the pollen and dander from the air that triggered my asthma. The crispness of the air would stimulate the neurons within my brain, as the thirst for knowledge was being fed to me through the words I read from many books. Often on that blanket, lying in the green soft amongst the pines, I would dream. I'd dream of a better life for me, my brothers, and my sisters. I would dream of having the ability to eat hot meals consisting of the finest foods three times a day. I would dream of family vacations to the beaches with white sand, and birds chirping with serene intent. I would dream of sitting beside another man who was not my father as he would tell me stories about his childhood, or have him tell me how much he loved me.

Dreams of being wanted and cared for.

Dreams of being treated with respect and honor.

Those dreams seemed so far-fetched and so unrealistic. Yet, I still prayed to God that he would bring those lucid dreams to my conscious reality. Those dreams never came to fruition for me. It was just me and the "Devil" trying to survive until the next day. That's all I could do. I was powerless. Has my life been destined for failure?

What is the fault in my stars? Through all the pain and the hopes of my dreams, I always told myself, they won't break me, they will not kill me. I am a survivor. I will not yield!

CHAPTER SEVEN

Sweet Cigar Smoke

God,

Please deliver me from bondage. The pain is too much for me to handle. I don't think I'll be able to make it. Today, I attempted to take all the pain pills in my mother's bathroom, but I threw up most of them immediately. I wanted to die. I'm so scared for myself. I'm so scared for my brothers and sisters. Please save me! Please save us!

Amen

Like all the other days after the morning summer showers had come, I quickly grabbed my encyclopedia Britannica and blanket and rushed to my secret hideaway beyond the piney woods. On this day, I noticed it was a bit windier than usual. The trees rustled and swayed back and forth, making a beautiful, joyous noise that played in complete concert with the heavens above. As the morning breeze blew, the smell from the tree leaves painted the air effortlessly, just as Michelangelo's brush painted the canvas of the Sistine Chapel. The chilliness of the air proved too much for my bare skin. I tightly wrapped myself up in my blanket and began my studies. On this day, I was reading and learning about World War II and how a large portion of the world was at the mercy of a conqueror named Hitler.

The unfamiliar, unpredictable, windy, and cool morning temperatures made me rather drowsy. Before I knew it, I was sound asleep with the encyclopedia still within the grasp of my hands. The dampness of the grass provided a cool sensation to my body, as if I were floating in the confines of the Pacific Ocean. I often imagined waves striking my face, as my body would be bounced and tossed by their peaks and crests. The wind howled amongst the treetops as I gently slept the morning away. Somehow, I knew this day would be different from the others I experienced in my special place beyond the pines.

Suddenly, the peaceful sleep I was experiencing was slightly interrupted by a feeling I had never experienced before. An intense sensation of safety and protection enveloped me. This feeling was strong and prompted me to want to wake up. But I momentarily ignored the feeling until it could no longer go unheeded. As I lay there, now partially conscious, I heard Him call my name. He usually wouldn't wake me from my sleep, but we had a special relationship. I had no issue responding to his call.

"Yes, sir, what's up?"

"Open your eyes, my son." I wondered why he would wake me, knowing this sleep was better than I received at home?

He called again, "My son, it's time for you to rise. I have something to show you."

I yawned and stretched my hands in preparation to wake up. I knew I had to tend to whatever this "Devil" desired. As I partially opened my eyes, I became frozen in astonishment at what I witnessed.

There He stood at the base of my feet. I completely blocked out everything around me, as my mind was only able to focus on the presence that stood before me. My arms erupted into goosebumps as the air temperature suddenly dropped. There He stood. The voice in my head had now materialized right before my eyes. His body was completely rigid as the newly rising sun was over his right shoulder.

He appeared to be around six feet five inches or even taller. I couldn't really tell for sure since I was lying down flat on my back looking up. He was dressed as you would see a man from the South around the 1940s; the suit He wore was just a dash too big for him, especially the jacket. Overall, the suit looked more like it had been handed down by a family member who was almost thirty pounds heavier than He. That's our tradition in the South – passing on clothes to the next generation. Even though the clothes might not fit the recipient immediately, there was room for them to grow into them. If holes and rips appeared, they were usually patched up so they could be worn even more, and continued to be passed down.

The "Devil" also wore this unusual hat. I couldn't place where I had seen such a headdress before, but it was odd. It was black, had a unique shine, and was completely oversized for his head. His hat kind of reminded me of the same top hat that the Planters peanut character wore on TV commercials. The all black Top hat. That top hat was perfectly situated on his head, whereas I couldn't make out an accurate description of his face. If there was one thing I distinctly remember from my first encounter with Him, it was his smell. I think back to that day, and recall that it wasn't his distinct words from his voice that had awakened me, but the sweet smell of cigar smoke that made me rise. I couldn't recall if He actually was pulling and puffing on an actual cigar, but He carried the scent as if he had just smoked moments before appearing to me.

His first words confused me once I became completely conscious after my sleep. He said, "Don't go to the house, just run. Run to the neighbor's and call your grandmother to come and pick you up." I was confused by the words I just heard.

I asked hesitantly, "What do you mean?"

He responded abruptly, "Listen, my son. Don't respond to his voice. Don't go to the house…Run! Tell your grandmother to come and get you now."

I became frightened and started to sob in fear. At that moment, I was confused because I didn't hear anyone else's voice besides His own. There wasn't anyone calling me. What is He talking about? This was the first time His words were frightening to me. I closed my eyes to wipe the streaming tears from my face, and when they reopened, He was out of sight. I could no longer see his hat, the suit, or smell the scent of the cigar. I looked all about the area in which I lay to no avail. He had vanished. I took a deep breath again to clear my mind and ease the fear of the quite unusual experience I just had. I sat there, lost in thought, trying to understand the words he meant.

Suddenly, a voice echoed across the bushes, gaining my full attention. This voice was not that of my "Devil," but the chilling voice of my father. I gathered my book and blanket and briskly walked back to the house. As I walked, I noticed I had been in the field longer than usual. I wasn't sure of the exact time, but it felt closer to the afternoon than morning. Where had the hours gone? The loss of time while I was on the blanket was entirely unexplainable for me at this point. What happened to me? I was also contemplating why He told me to run away and call Grandmother. I approached the front door of my home and tucked the blanket and book out of sight to the side of the house so he wouldn't see me walking in with them. As I walked through the door, he stood angrily there. God help me, I whispered a prayer that only I could hear. I know why the "Devil" told me to run. I approached my Father, my brother was already in tears, and answered, "Yes, sir?"

"Where's my fucking money? You steal from me nigga? I'm missing twenty dollars from my pocket. Which one of y'all greedy, no count mother fuckers stole it from me? And where the fuck you been, I was looking for you almost an hour ago!" Soon after he questioned us, he disappeared for about five minutes or so. The anticipation of what was to come instantly made my stomach turn in knots. He returned to the same place where he had summoned us with an unforgettable scowl across his face.

There he stood with a wooden stick in his hand. Apparently, he had broken off the broom handle in preparation for punishing me and my brother. Usually, we wouldn't get the broom handle, so this had to be a special occasion. This weapon of choice came from an old broom we stopped using for chores almost three months earlier. I wanted to put it out for the trash, but somehow kept forgetting to do it. My negligence had come back to haunt me on that day.

As our beating commenced, it seemed like it was a free-for-all on our bodies. Every limb, every phalange, every joint was assaulted with malicious intent. He lashed every part of me and my brother with that broom handle. My hands, feet, ass, face, arms and back were all subjected to pain and punishment on that day. He wielded the broom handle against my frail frame just as a Templar knight would have brandished his sword to defend the Pope's greatest secrets. This beating lasted for about thirteen minutes as my mother gazed and smiled from her bedroom door.

Blow after blow, she looked on at the beatings as if she were Caesar, enjoying the gladiator matches from ancient Rome, waiting for blood to be spilled. We cried out to our mother for help, but the smile on her face let us know she wouldn't help. Our sobs and pleas only fell upon her deaf ears. She turned her back on us that late Spring morning. Perhaps it was a brief respite from the beatings she received that left her feeling pleased and amused. Or maybe our cries of desperation and hopelessness ringing in her eardrums proved too much for her tolerance.

Regardless, the eruptions from the broomstick were now causing the pain to course through every part of my frail body. After he stopped, we hobbled to our rooms to finish crying and lick our wounds. Paralyzed by grief and sorrow, that night I gave a pleading, desperate prayer to my God in Heaven. I knew that in my mind, this would be it, my last attempt at getting a response from Him. Why wouldn't He help me? I asked myself. I opened my eyes after the verbal dedication and adjusted my homemade ice pack to fit better over my right eye. I could taste and feel the warm blood in my mouth and the back of my throat. I wasn't sure if I had bitten my tongue or the broom handle had broken a blood vessel in my mouth.

Regardless, I lay there and wondered if this was the punishment that Judas had to endure for his betrayal of Christ. I was thankful that it wasn't 100 dollars missing; maybe he would have killed us. By the end of my self-contemplation, the room seemed to grow about ten degrees colder as I rolled and tucked my body under the blanket on my bed.

My head then began to spin a hundred miles per hour as nausea set in. My body could no longer withstand the punishment I had just received. As I lay in my bed, I could barely hold the tears back as my body violently shook and shivered. I couldn't explain why I was shaking so hard; this had never happened before. Suddenly, I leaned over the side of the bed and threw up the contents of my stomach. Even though I hadn't been eating much, whatever was on my stomach that day ended up on my bedroom floor. The pain grew unbearable as my head pounded from the strikes of the broomstick across my skull. Then, without any prompt or warning, darkness became my friend. I lay there unconscious from my wounds and pain. During my period of oblivion, He appeared. He scolded me for not listening to him. "I told you not to go to the house, but you didn't follow my instructions."

"No more prayers to God, my son. He doesn't want to hear you! Call me. Call me, I say!" I was not frightened by his tone because I knew I wouldn't be in pain if I had listened. "Whenever you feel threatened or fearful, call out my name." He paused to drag on his cigar, then addressed me once more. "I will protect you, my son, under any circumstances. I will protect you. Just call my name when in need, and I will be there." As the cigar smoke intensified, a deep, unwanted silence descended upon them.

A certain peace beseeched my body and my mind. He then spoke in a whisper, so ever gently in my ear, "Open your eyes, awake my son. I am here to serve you and guide you throughout this life. My son, may my name be at your service and peace for you in times of peril. May my name be the calm in the midst of your storm. May my name echo the sounds of peace and protection. May my name bring you the power to vanquish your enemies, for revenge rests on your very lips. My name, the name you should never forget, I am Shemyaza."

CHAPTER EIGHT

School Days

Dear God,

Why are these days so long? I really thank you for my grandmother, she is a true angel. Do you hear my prayers? If you do, please respond. I need you in my life so badly. Is this life you have given me real? When will your rain stop?

The following morning, I woke up bruised and battered, but alive. My legs and back ached so badly from the assault with the broomstick. To my knowledge, he never found the twenty dollars that he claimed were missing from his pants pocket. My lower back was so sore that I couldn't sit directly up, and I even had to roll over on my side to get out of bed. I knew at that moment it was clear I wouldn't be able to dress for gym the next school day with all the scars, lacerations, and bruises on my body. If someone were to see that carnage, they would call the police and have my parents arrested. Hopefully, even though part of me wanted that to happen very badly, I couldn't predict what would happen to us if they went to jail. After managing to get out of bed, I realized it would be a challenge to sit down on the bus, and even a greater feat to sit down in a classroom desk.

As I rose that morning, part of the love I had for my brother was now missing. I resented him for some reason. I knew I didn't take that money. The only question now was whether my brother had taken it. So, either my father was lying, or my brother took the money. He didn't confess, so I would never know for sure. In my gut, I felt he was too frightened to admit it. Regardless, we got one of the worst beatings of our life because of twenty fucking dollars. I felt like a punching bag used in training camp for a prize fighter. He beat us like he hated us, and all over twenty dollars. My father showed us that even the smallest amount of money was more important than the well-being of his children.

I showered shortly after getting up and eating a piece of toast for breakfast. That's the only thing we had in the house that was edible. As usual, I was hungry when I arrived at school.

I took my clothes off and looked in the mirror at the damage that was on my body. My eyes watered with tears, even though the beating had transpired the day prior. I was emotionally distraught from the sight of the wounds, and even as the tears flowed down my face, I knew I must remain strong. I was not going to allow this to break me. After stepping into the shower, the hot water hit my flesh, and seemed to agitate the bruises and cuts even more. It was so fucking painful. Why does soap have to hurt so bad! I rushed from the shower and dressed before the bus came.

The cool, moist air from the early morning seemed to help relieve the stinging as I stood on the side of the road waiting for my bus. Riding the bus was always a challenge for my siblings and me. The neighborhood kids would always joke at us. Whether on the bus or at school, they always talked badly about us. We were the easy targets of many jokes. They always teased us about our names, religion, and whatever happened in our house. For some odd reason, they always seemed to know what was going on in our home. They could tell if I got beaten or if my mother got beaten up. It always seemed like I was in the counselor's office to have a conversation. She really didn't give a fuck about me, or what was going on inside me. I felt like she was one of the people spreading the gossip and rumors. After a while, I stopped going altogether. There was really no point because if God wasn't stepping in to stop the abomination of my father's fists, then nobody was.

Even though the kids clowned us, school was another place of refuge. I would often cry when I had a moment alone to myself. The crying would help relieve the stress and frustration inside me. I often wondered why we were targets, but people seemed to seek us out for unknown reasons.

People I didn't even know would come up and just stare at me for no reason. I felt like I had a hideous mark or scar upon my face that people couldn't help but gaze upon. It seemed that whenever people needed to release stress or wanted to feel better, they found us. The insults would come like raindrops during a spring thunderstorm – heavily and swiftly.

Eventually I learned to stop crying and learned to talk hard core shit back at the bullies. I was good at talking shit about fucking people's mommas. Let me tell it, I was putting my dick in everybody's mother in the neighborhood. "Yeah nigga, after your daddy left for work, I crept through the back door fucked the shit out your momma real hard," I would often say. Mother's jokes were always the best. Regardless of whether the kids liked you, everybody laughed at a good joke.

I talked crazy shit about the fat ass fathers, too. All the parents in my neighborhood were at least fifty pounds overweight, and I was very good at making that very well known. My infamous line after every joke was, "Fuck your fat ass mother-fucking daddy nigga."

The word mother-fucker became a large part of my vocabulary. Although I didn't use the word at home, I sure as hell used it in school, and I used it all the time. At the lunch table, it was the word mother-fucker. On the playground, it was the word mother-fucker, in the classroom it was non-stop mother-fucker. I used the word mother-fucker so much, I even called my teacher motherfucker.

"Excuse me Mrs. Motherfucker, can I go to the restroom?"

"Yes, and take your ass and your books to detention on the way," the teacher replied.

"Thank you, Mrs. Motherfucker," I would say back in complete laughter. I was out of control and downright disrespectful. All of my disrespectful actions were intended in jest and also served as a deflection tool to keep the bullies at bay. I just wanted to try to fit in and keep people talking about what I did in school, in comparison to the rumors about what was happening inside my home. Besides receiving detention or being sent to the principal's office, the joking would often escalate into fights after school, and sometimes even during school.

It was fun sometimes, but more importantly, I gained more respect and was able to eat regularly. My mother never made breakfast for us during the week, only occasionally on the weekends. Upon reflection, breakfast had to be my favorite meal of the day. It was also very easy to get leftovers that weren't served in the cafeteria, since many of the kids showed up late to school. My grandmother and great aunt worked in the kitchen, so I always loaded up on whatever they served for the day. They always cooked and served the best breakfast. I'm talking about sausage, pancakes, French toast, bacon, and, my personal favorite, grits and eggs.

Although the religion of my parents prohibited me from eating pork, the sausage and biscuits served in the cafeteria were off the chain. Every chance I got, I overindulged on pork products against my parents' knowledge. I didn't fully understand the aspects of the Islamic religion, but that bacon and sausage sure did taste really good. Why was something so forbidden so good? I loved the swine, and the swine loved me back. I was in complete rebellion mode. Anything my parents preached and stood for, I defied. But I learned the spirit of defiance from them. I often listened to them when they engaged in conversation about politics and other social issues. One of their most talked-about subjects was racial disparities in Alabama and how it should be legal to smoke marijuana.

In fact, that's all they talked about while smoking their marijuana – the White man. Let them tell it, the White man was to blame for the sky being blue. I often fantasized about antagonizing my parents by coming home with a ham and egg sandwich on white bread and the big-breasted White girl off the TV show Baywatch. As I remember, it was several sets of big breasts on that show, and I loved them all. The sight of that would really piss them off, and I would be more than happy doing it!

Besides the forbidden pork products in school, I loved the dynamic science and math classes my teachers provided. Of the two, math was my favorite. I got very good at solving math equations that most kids would struggle with. I often competed in math tournaments that the school held in competition with other area schools. These competitions were fun and very competitive, even though I never placed higher than 6th. To me, that wasn't half bad for a country boy with limited resources and a turbulent household.

Science and math were the subjects that always prompted me to think beyond my normal realms of understanding. For me, it's always about trying to predict what's next. As a kid, I learned to think and process information at a competitive rate. Sometimes, I would get disheartened in class because the teacher couldn't always answer my questions. I wasn't being a smart ass when I asked them, but I was always somehow punished for even the most innocent curiosities. Naturally, I would stop asking questions in class as my confidence declined. School no longer provided a safe haven as my home's troubles grew more turbulent. The walls of my only refuge were slowly crumbling around me as the beatings at home rapidly increased. Slowly but surely, my grades declined, and I lost much interest in my school studies.

By the time I finished the 9th grade, the concept of school and maintaining a high academic standard was out the door. I noticed that my urge to socialize was fading fast. The few friends I had were busy with social activities, such as school clubs, athletics, and, most importantly, girls. The most social time I've ever had was attending school basketball and football games. Most of my free time was spent at home watching my favorite TV shows.

The television was somewhat of a secret asylum and refuge since I lacked the confidence and basic social skills to be comfortable in public. One of my greatest fears was having to interact with my peers. My peers would often discuss what their mothers were cooking for dinner. It reminded me that I was probably gonna have grits and boiled eggs. The kids would always talk about fun things they planned for the weekend. For me, it was no fun plans, just being in that house of horrors. Other than attending the occasional football game, I was home. More importantly, my male peers mostly talked about girls.

I loved to talk about girls! I loved seeing girls! I loved the very thought of anything having to do with girls. My hormones were starting to kick in during my sophomore year of high school, and I noticed a lot about girls. I loved the way girls talked and licked their lips. The shapelier girls with thick, juicy lips and shapely thighs caught my attention often. I would frequently fantasize about some of my female classmates, wondering what it would be like to date some of them. I often wondered how nice it would be to talk on the phone or even go to the movies with someone equally interested in me as I was in them.

Even while hanging with my friends in the neighborhood, I talked about how many girls I would speak to in school. Everybody and their mama knew I wasn't talking to no damn girls, and I didn't have any phone numbers to prove the bullshit I was talking. My neighborhood pals and I would often sit around and bet who was going to fuck a girl, or ever get her phone number. I was always on the losing end of many bets. Most of the time, my losing bets came from not even trying. I lacked the confidence to approach the girls I liked. What made things worse was that of the girls I found attractive, the majority were usually the ones who made jokes about me when I entered the cafeteria. Listening to the guys talk about their experiences with girls made me want to take a different approach to getting a girlfriend. My friends would always say that their dads, uncles, and other older relatives in their family would share tips on how to talk to and attract women. This made me despise my father even more because he never spoke one word to me about girls, let alone share advice about them with me.

Girls, girls, and more girls occupied my thoughts and consciousness. I often fantasized about having a girlfriend, but I knew it would be a distant reality. What could I do to get a girl to notice me?

The summer of my freshman year, as I transitioned to 10th grade, brought new ideas and approaches to solving my most elusive problem: finding a girlfriend. I realized that I needed to dress like the other kids. I needed a new wardrobe and a new haircut. I figured I needed a new attitude to get the girls I wanted. So, without even being out of school for a week, I started my very first job. I followed Dawn's footsteps and was hired at the local Hardee's fast food restaurant. As soon as I got hired, they put me in the most feared position in the whole job, the drive-thru. I had to be fast, accurate, and, more importantly, talk to people all day long.

Why couldn't I be just on fries, or on the cleanup crew, I often thought.

According to my thought processes, the money I made would give me an opportunity to attract the attention I desperately needed. I mean, that's what I saw in the movies. Guys with all the money and the flashy clothes always had the pretty girls. That summer, I even developed the first concept of what I thought the ideal woman should look like. In my mind, I figured I deserved a woman who would have respected me for my intelligence and sensitivity. I used to visualize myself and my special lady attending the opera in a big city like Los Angeles or New York. My fantasy involved me and that special lady stepping out of a Lamborghini in complete style and confidence. I would don a black and white tuxedo with a nice Rolex watch to complement my evening attire. She would have a beautiful light blue or black evening gown to complement her radiant, medium-brown skin. She would have on high heels that would make her approximately three inches taller than my 5'11" frame. Her hair would be soft, silky, and brown, falling perfectly on the cusp of her shoulders.

My ideal woman would have to wait several years because that four dollars and twenty-five cents an hour job I had wouldn't suffice for the dreams I possessed. I could barely get the girls at my high school to speak to me, much less be the woman I fantasized about. My plan for that summer was to work hard and save as much of my money as I could. I knew that to get the clothes I wanted, I needed to save and buy them for myself. I already knew that my parents weren't going to buy shit for me. Although I couldn't accurately predict how much I would bring home after taxes, I set a clear and precise goal of saving $750.

Working in the fast food industry was arduous and fast-paced. Most of the time, I worked 14-hour shifts. My feet were often weary and sore by the end of the day, but I pressed on. Working at Hardee's served a greater purpose than the money. It kept me out of the house for long periods. I often thought that if I were not at home, I could avoid the stress my parents caused. The very notion of employment made that very tiring and woeful job a complete blessing, making it easier to endure. I would even work for people who wanted to take days off to go out to the club or be with their family. Receiving a paycheck every other Friday was one of the best aspects of my job; however, there was a drawback to working in the customer service industry.

Alabama presented certain challenges within itself regarding race relations and customer service. Some White people felt they could speak to me in any manner. I was called everything from "coon" to "boy." I distinctly recall being called a nigger on several occasions while taking orders from the drive through. At the pinnacle of disrespect, I had a Coke thrown in my face by a truck full of white boys who were upset about their order being incorrect.

They ordered a Coke, and I had given them a Sprite in my haste to expedite their order. My manager watched studiously as the Sprite splashed in my face and clothes. His obnoxious chuckle further let me know that he didn't really give a shit as he watched the truck speed off without a response from him. That wasn't the first or last time I was humiliated and disrespected by ignorant ass people at that lonely drive-thru window; but through it all, I stood tall in the midst of their abhorrence and ill wills. My plans of independence and financial freedoms superseded their means of demoralization. I willed myself to achieve the goal of $750.

By the end of the summer, it was time to finally harvest the fruits of my labor. As I reached under my mattress to pull out the dirty gym socks I used to keep my money, I called upon my friend Shemyaza.

I asked, "What am I to do if I don't have the amount of money I set out to save?"

He responded, "Nothing, my son, just work harder. I am so proud of you! This is just the beginning for you." At the end of the first counting session, a feeling of disbelief lingered within my spirit. So, I started counting a second time, just to be sure my math skills hadn't suddenly taken a turn for the worse. Each time I got closer to the end of the stack of paper bills, my heart thumped with excitement.

At the end of the third time, I was in utter shock at the amount. All three times yielded the same amount. The feeling of satisfaction and accomplishment raced through my heart and mind. I did it and then some! I saved almost 1300 dollars, nearly twice the amount I had set out to save. The following weekend, I went and purchased new clothes for the upcoming school year. I thought I was doing it big. The highlight of my newly purchased wardrobe was the new MC Hammer pants, the patent leather shoes, and the matching shirt. With my new garments within my grasp, I gained a renewed sense of accomplishment. As hard as it was, with many obstacles presented on my path, I overcame them all. I did what I said I would do! I am so proud of myself!

Ultimately, with my new clothes and newfound sense of superficial confidence, I had successfully created a new persona. The severe beatings my parents gave me had shattered my self-esteem, but I hid my lack of self-esteem behind my new and shiny material things. Just as the morning produces a new risen sun, so did I. I created a new person altogether. I had the entity who called itself Shemyaza on my side; I possessed new clothes and a shallow confidence that was only on the exterior.

I decided that summer that I would no longer subject myself to my parents' abuse. I was ready to fight for my life at all costs. No longer shall I be weak and beg for their help; I had Shemyaza for that. Thanks to my accomplishments and new perspectives on life, I decided not to be held within the confines of religion and its laws. God's framework and grand designs no longer fit the framework of my life. To me, there was no point to the concept of sin. Why did sin even exist? I decided within the temple of my mind that the God I was taught about could not be all-powerful.

If this God were all-powerful, why did He ignore my devotion to Him and just watch me get degraded and reduced to nothing? I eventually figured that if He, God, was all-powerful, He couldn't have been just a God of good deeds, as religious books described Him. That summer I became anew, reborn, and resurrected. The concept of God I was taught was quickly placed in the dark. No longer shall I carry the cross of abuse and neglect. I will no longer serve any master but myself! I am the master of my destiny and the chief of my soul. I am the creator of my reality!

CHAPTER NINE

Revelations

Now that I was somewhat restored to life, I no longer wanted to be seen as a weak and unsure little boy. I had a stride about my walk, just as an upright and enlightened man should. I was now armed with a new knowledge of myself and a new sense of purpose. I walked, talked, and even thought differently. Turmoil and violence reached their peaks in my home, but I found a way to keep the negativity at bay. One of the ways I kept balance was by reading the Bible. For a Muslim to read the Bible was, at the very least, odd; however, I was intrigued by the apparent, intentional mathematical references I found within it.

For example, the Book of Psalms is divided into five major sections.

In addition to the number 5, the number 12 is also heavily immersed in the foundation of the Bible. The more I read on a daily basis, the more I discovered an emphasis on specific numbers, and I felt compelled to unveil the true meaning behind those numbers. 5 and 12 are so significant throughout the Word of God, but none more important than the significance of those numbers placed inside the illustrious Book of Revelation.

Every time I read the Book of Revelations, it gave me hope that all the abuse and drama would end one day. Just as this specific Bible story professed hell and brimstone, there was another revelation that would send major ripples of hatred and disgust through my family. A revelation that was supposed to be kept a secret from all those who were not deemed worthy of knowing, but this secret was too big to be hidden from those who sought clarity through truth and the light. A secret that would continue to grow for months, but eventually this hidden truth would take on a life of its own.

I often wondered why the beatings in my house hit an apex, and then completely flat-lined. Trust me, at this point of my life I wasn't going to complain at all about not getting my ass kicked. Yet, suddenly, all the beatings just completely stopped out of the blue. Why? Something was different in my house, and I couldn't figure out exactly what that was. The energy had completely shifted. The veil of oppression and abuse had not lifted, but something was so different in my house. I recall reading about Sir Isaac Newton's Laws of Physics and the conservation of energy in the encyclopedias. "Energy is neither created nor destroyed; it merely changes form." In my attempt to apply these physical laws to my chaotic life, I figured if we weren't getting beat up as much, then my father's energy and frustration were being exerted somewhere else. But, where?

One morning, when all was peaceful, I summoned Shemyaza for enlightenment and wisdom. As always, He appeared upon my request with the ubiquitous smell of sweet cigar smoke. I asked Him why the energy in my home had changed to the point where it was peaceful and serene, compared to its previously hellish nature. The change was so sudden, it reminded me of the peaceful nature of a hurricane's eye. And just like the eye of a cyclone approaching landfall, what followed the eye was the worst part of the storm.

I ultimately asked Shemyaza whether he was responsible for our apparent deliverance, but I was left feeling that he was not the accountable party. Shemyaza spoke that morning in a tone I had never heard from Him. He spoke in circles and used codes that were unfamiliar to my rationale. I couldn't quite decipher the meaning of his words on that brisk fall morning, but His tone left me very uneasy.

Shemyaza boldly stated, "Rise, embrace the darkness, my son, and the light shall be revealed to you."

I had no idea what his words meant, but I became more watchful of everyone in my home. Was someone leaving or moving out? Did my parents become happy again? Was someone sick? These hypotheses constantly ran through my mind as I attempted to figure out the transition in my home. Shemyaza's words consistently resonated in the deep recesses of my brain,

"Rise, embrace the darkness, my son, and the light shall be revealed to you." What was to come of all this? Why were his words so shrouded in secrecy?

After about three weeks, I gave up trying to figure out why things were happening the way they were and just enjoyed the fact that there was less stress in my home. I didn't receive an ass whooping in almost a month. I had money in my pocket, some decent shoes, and clothes on my back. All the feelings of bliss and comfort changed one late Friday night, causing my little world to collapse completely at its core.

Just as most young men do, I often would get up at night, and go to the bathroom for an early morning piss. On that chilly pre-dusk morning, I awoke from my sleep only to lie there for a second just to gather my faculties and prepare myself for the trip to the bathroom. Right before rolling out of bed, I heard the distinct sound of a man urinating, followed immediately by the toilet flushing. I didn't give it a second thought at that moment, but it seemed odd. My younger brother and I were the only ones who would get up in the middle of the night to go pee. I looked to the bed on the other side of the room where my brother slept, and he lay there peacefully. So, in my mind, I knew it wasn't him. I also knew that my father's bathroom was inside their room.

Then the footsteps.

The footsteps were walking back towards my parents' room. The footsteps of my father. I knew those footsteps from anywhere. But why was he walking so softly, as if he cared enough not to walk his normal heavy-footed step and wake us up? We had many plumbing problems, so it's possible that their toilet was broken and he had to use our bathroom. As I rose from my bed, my morning release was interrupted by yet another flushing of the toilet, followed by the sound of the shower turning on.

Who was in the shower at 4 am? Why are they in the shower at this hour? Is my clock wrong, or is someone getting ready for work? It's a Saturday morning... no one goes to work on a Saturday. I smelled the comforting scent of Shemyaza's cigar, so I knew that I was protected during my inquisition period. I peeped around the corner of my bedroom door just enough so that I couldn't be seen. Who was in this damn shower this early and why? As the shower stopped, I looked at the bathroom door in blurry vision. My oldest sister, Dawn, appeared from the steamy door and rushed back to her room. With my mind in all-out confusion, I went to the bathroom, quickly urinated, and returned to my room.

Now I was beginning to wonder about what was happening before my eyes. I didn't want to get angry for no reason at all. I wasn't sure exactly what I saw, but I knew something in my gut didn't feel right. Perhaps it was just a bad dream, and none of this was happening. Maybe it was my mind playing tricks on me, and this was all a weird coincidence. Regardless, I heeded Shemyaza's words of embracing the dark.

Later that morning, after breakfast, I took to my secret place just beyond the pines to assemble my thoughts. I was too scared to ask my sister why she took a shower so soon before sunrise in such a clandestine manner. I chose to keep my inquiries to myself for the time being and sleep lightly for the next couple of weeks. For my peace of mind, I wanted to know that this was all a coincidence. I needed to understand if there was a method to her madness of early morning showers. I mean, after all, there were seven children in the house, and the hot water was minimal. Not to mention, my mother and father took showers as well. So maybe Dawn was showering before everyone else to ensure she got plenty of hot water and enough time to enjoy her shower.

That appeased my mind for that moment, but the very essence of my soul felt that something else much bigger was happening. The whole idea of me playing private detective seemed odd and creepy, but I trusted in Shemyaza. He hadn't ever lied to me, nor had He been incorrect about his statements... but there was this suppressing feeling of heaviness and dense sadness. I felt there was a major storm just beyond the horizon of my life.

From my early morning observations, my sister's morning showers lasted approximately two months. Seemingly enough, my Father cautiously used our bathroom for the next few weeks. His silent trips up the hall seemed to increase in time and frequency. I wanted to come and ask him if there was something wrong with his toilet, but I was afraid it would lead to an ass whooping. In addition, I felt that if I had asked him, it would tip him off that I was watching him. Consequently, if he knew of my observations, that would hinder my amateur investigation. So, I watched patiently and observed with the intent of solving this mystery.

Shemyaza would repeat His words without any emotion whatsoever, daily. Like a fucking tape recorder, He'd repeat the exact words all the time. "Embrace the dark, and the light will be revealed to you," and nothing else. Early one morning, I got up to use the bathroom as usual, and there he was. Sitting quietly on the edge of my bed, awaiting my return to consciousness. I would normally summon Shemyaza, but not on this day. As I cleared the mucus from my eyes, He stood and pointed to the door as if he knew I was ready to relieve my bladder.

Upon approaching the bedroom door, he harshly grabbed me by the shoulder as if to pause my movement. He placed his finger over his dry lips to indicate to me to be silent in my movements. I was nervous and uneasy about what he wanted me to see. As my heart pounded viciously in my chest cavity, I peeked around the corner, but saw nothing unusual. Everything appeared peaceful and serene, as early morning hours usually are. I took a glance back at the clock that sat on the small dusty bedroom dresser, and its red numbers

read 3:33. Damn, I thought to myself. This was not my usual hour of waking up to use the bathroom. I should still be asleep, but it was almost thirty minutes earlier.

I couldn't understand why Shemyaza was having me patiently and silently wait at my door in the complete cover of darkness. Then, what was revealed to me was that all Shemyaza's words had been put into motion. With my door slightly ajar, I observed who I called my father tiptoeing down the hallway and slowly yet cautiously entering my sister's room. Those soft and secretive footsteps yet again. The five steps he took to get to my sister's room. I hated that sound of his squeaky clandestine intent. Upon entering her room, I heard the lock gently click into place as he closed the door behind him. At that moment, my heart felt like it sank to the pits of my abdomen. For 12 minutes, I waited for him; finally, he left her room, as if he were justified in his actions.

All I could think of was that this was my sister, and that my father was violating her. I was a witness to my father raping my oldest sister right before my eyes. I could only think that she was fifteen years old! That's your daughter, you sick son of a bitch! Fuck You! So many questions and feelings of anger were running through my mind. So many emotions were coursing throughout my heart and veins upon my ghastly revelations. Part of me wanted to run and kick that door down and beat the shit out of my father. Yet, there was a part of me that wanted to run to my mother and tell her exactly what I had seen.

Unfortunately, I did neither. I thought I didn't have a chance of beating my father in a fight, and my gut feeling told me that my mother already knew about what was happening. Regardless, I walked with that very burden upon my shoulders. It shouldn't have mattered if I were a child or not; I failed to act. I would always wonder why I didn't say or do anything. In fact, I asked myself that question every day for several years. Why did I allow that to happen?

Why?

As the next several months passed, I withdrew from the few social activities I had been participating in. I only wanted to stay home and not face anyone and the rumors. After the devastating revelation, my grades became an afterthought, even more so than before, as the time I spent in the woods on my blanket increased.

The results of my father's transgressions were now on display for all to see, and my sister was his canvas. This was one of the lowest points of my life, having to hear about what was happening in my home. To me, it seemed as if either my mother knew about the heinous acts or she didn't care. Or she was so selfish in trying to maintain her reputation instead of getting my father arrested and protecting her kids. People damn well knew my sister didn't have a boyfriend, and that my father was having his way with her. How the fuck could my mother not know this was happening right under her nose?

Regardless, my sister's stomach continued to grow and expand on a weekly and monthly basis. The child she carried was a direct result of continuous rape and sexual abuse. No one seemed to care about what was occurring in my house, not even the God I worshipped. How could God be so highly praised as being omnipotent and omnipresent, and yet God sat back and watched His children beaten and raped? Does He hear my prayers? Does He not listen to me plead? Why doesn't He answer me? How am I not supposed to hate my father? Is this child to be my brother/sister or my nephew/niece? How the fuck is her stomach getting big as hell, and my mother not notice shit?! Maybe it was I who was to stop the abuse in my home. Perhaps it was my destiny to end the war between the darkness and the light. Was I to stop the monster who roamed the hallways looking for the innocence to feed his hunger?

Per the King James Bible, the Lord God states, "Dearly beloved, avenge not yourselves, but rather give place unto wrath: for it is written, Vengeance is mine; I will repay, sayeth the Lord." I decided that my father will not have to wait until the Lord passes judgment on the world, nor must he wait till the rapture, as the Book of Revelations speaks of. The reign of his tyranny, violence, and abuse shall end by the force of my mighty hand. My face will be the last face he sees. I will be, I shall be, my father's reckoning.

CHAPTER TEN

The Plot

At the end of her third trimester, my sister was forced to deliver a child she carried for 10 months. A child resulting from the cruelest act of betrayal and moral transgression. Subsequently, she had to give up that very child for adoption. Watching my sister carry a child that was my father's made me furious. Even during her pregnancy, he repeatedly raped and abused her without remorse. He was an animal without a conscience, feasting and preying upon the weak.

I knew it was time for me to act. I had to seize control of my life. I had to become the determining factor for my present and the future of my brothers and sisters. So that evening, after learning of the child's birth, I rested quietly in my bed in preparation for sleep. I summoned Shemyaza to share my judgments and feelings of anger and hatred. I felt his advice was warranted that evening, as my mind pondered and conjured a master plot.

By simply saying his name, He would humbly appear at my request. After calling his name every so quietly, he seemed to sit soundlessly on the corner of my sheetless mattress. "Why have you summoned me on this evening, my son?" I lay there gently gathering my thoughts, unsure of what to say and how to say it. Shemyaza broke the silence by saying, "What do you request, my son?"

I quickly answered, "I'm tired of this motherfucker! I hate this nigga man! Enough of his bullshit!"

"My son, be aware of what you control," he replied. There are only three things that you do: your thoughts, your emotions, and your actions are all in your power and control. My son, most importantly, you must be aware of your actions. There will be and shall be consequences for everything that you do. There are always equal and opposite reactions to your thoughts." It was almost as if He was reading my deepest and darkest thoughts. There was another long and monotonous pause as He watched me standing. As He seemingly drew from his cigar, the sweet-smelling smoke hit my nostrils, and in turn the smoke relaxed my eyelids even more so than before.

By the time I closed my eyes, my thoughts were a bewildering and confused mess. I wanted to contemplate them even further, but the forcefulness of sleep overcame me. As I lay there with my eyes shut, I could hear Shemyaza softly whisper in my ear, "Do what thou please. Do what thy heart desires."

* * * * *

The new rising sun prompted me to open my eyes the following morning. I woke up fresh and rejuvenated from the peaceful sleep. I lay there in a very tranquil state and realized I had decided how to seize control of my family's future—all of the years of abuse and pain had finally come to an apex. I knew immediately that there would be a climactic moment that would lead to an ultimate sacrifice. Without hesitation, secret evasion, or mental reservation, this magic moment would lead me and my father on a collision course so violent that only one of us would survive. For me to rid my family of the pain and discourse, this plan must be followed through without fear. Never again will he hit me, my mother, or my brothers and sisters. Never again will he be allowed to rape another sister of mine. Never again will he be able to abandon any of us.

On that brisk spring morning, I decided to unleash a master plan that involved me killing my father. Neither Jesus nor Allah would return to reclaim his soul in a mythical rapture. He would never receive Archangel Michael's blessing and enter the pearly gates of

Heaven. No virgins, nor milk and honey as he believed—just darkness and pain from a brief moment in time with me, the "Devil" himself.

As the taste of revenge was on my lips, I began plotting the course that would change my life forever. My savior, Shemyaza, was the only one who knew of my master plan, even though he didn't speak of it. My plot was to be both masterful and sadistic. I wanted my father to feel the pain of all that he inflicted upon us. Since he was the author of so much pain and destruction, why not let him read the words from the very book he had written. Days after the birth of my sister's child, I saw him strutting around the house as if he were proud of a great accomplishment that had been recently completed.

As if he were the master builder who had just erected King Solomon's Temple, his energy and mere presence sickened me. The lust for revenge and the taste for his blood made my pupils dilate and my pulse quicken. I looked and glared at him with great disdain. Little did he know that in just a few days, his chickens would be coming home to roost, and I would be sitting in the chicken shack patiently waiting for him.

After about 3 days of deep thought, I finally figured out how he was going to die. It was going to happen on March 20th, the day and hour of the Spring Equinox. The books on ancient spiritual systems taught me that all great blood sacrifices would occur on the equinoxes and the solstices. I decided, why not? Let him be the Lamb, just as God directed Abraham to sacrifice Isaac. His blood shall spill as Abel's did by the hands of his brother, Cain. Let his blood flow as the first-born sons of Egypt slain by the Hebrew God. Let his blood stream and feed the earth as "First Father" from the Mayan culture. His blood was going to be my sacrifice, and those who came before me shall be pleased with my sweet offerings. So shall it be done.

65

My sacrifice was to be initiated at 11:59 on the evening of March 20th so that when the equinox came to fruition on the 21st, his blood would be fresh. The spirits of the morning could then feast upon his essence, which I had prepared for them.

Three days before the event, I had prepared a sword that he kept at home. I used a sharpening tool from the 4-H shop at school to ensure that the blade was prepared to slice the arteries in his neck with ease. I also had stolen my mother's 38 caliber snub nose pistol just in case the plan didn't go as planned. If there was a glitch, I could end it quickly with a shot to his head.

I wanted precision and accuracy for my special day of liberation. No mistakes. He will die at my hands. In addition to the gun and sword, I prepared my backpack with duct tape, gloves, a sock, and a fire poker.

Later that evening, my mother and father had a big fight as I was preparing for this event. At this point in their marriage, he would leave and stay with my grandmother for a couple of days until things cooled off. He always avoided being arrested by staying there, but my mother, stupidly enough, consciously allowed him back at home to do the same shit all over again. Just as I had planned, he left on a Thursday night, and I knew he would try to return by the following Sunday. I had to seize my window of opportunity and execute my offering to the Gods.

On that Friday evening, after school, I made a point to visit my grandmother to ensure he was staying there. Just like clockwork, I saw his bags in his room neatly beside his bed. Even though my grandmother had a guest bed in her house, he always chose to sleep in the room where he grew up. Unbeknownst to him, that very room where he experienced bliss and joy would be the same room in which he would take his last breath. That evening, I left the side door open so I could quickly and quietly gain access to my grandmother's house.

The side door would lead me straight to his room without any notice from anyone else in the house. I was confident that my plan was ready and flawless, just waiting to be put into action.

I returned home that Friday and lay in bed contemplating my thoughts and actions for the following evening. I was ready. I was excited to start a new life without my father. I would need all of my strength to strike that mighty blow to his skull and bring darkness all about his world. I lay there in complete solemnity and tranquility, and there He suddenly appeared.

Shemyaza.

I had not summoned Him, so I wondered how He had known to be present on the eve of such a glorious day.

The sweet cigar smell, as usual, put me into a deep sleep. I wondered why we didn't converse that evening, but I didn't worry. He knew what was to come from my dark actions. I awoke the next morning refreshed and prepared to follow through. That afternoon, I decided to take a nap around 5 p.m. and to get up at 8 p.m. in preparation for the event. I woke up from the nap feeling tense and jittery. It is time, I said to myself.

As I stood across the parking lot of the school, I could see my grandmother's house only a few yards away. I removed my shoes so that my transition to the house would be seamless. I walked to the side of the house without making a sound. I put gloves on my sweaty, nervous hands. I stood at the side door for a brief moment, took a deep breath, and placed my hand upon the door knob. I quickly and nervously thought, what if they locked the door? What if he's still up? I will be doomed. I closed my eyes and slightly attempted to turn the door handle, and as I had planned, the door opened as if it awaited my return.

With a slight thrust from my frail shoulders, I pushed it open cautiously. As I slowly entered the house, my eyes suddenly caught a glimpse of a small light in my peripheral vision. They had left the oven light on. My guiding "Light". The oven light provided all the illumination I needed. I felt that a flashlight would have been too alarming and could have awakened my father. I took a deep breath, and my knees buckled as I gazed at his bedroom door—one step toward his room as my heart thumped even more loudly than before.

Little did he know, the five steps he took to get to my sister's room were the same five steps I was taking to get to his. The more my heart pounded, the louder it seemed to be creating an alarm for the rest of the house to hear. No one heard my robust palpitations, just as no one heard the cries, the pleas, and screams as he pounded upon my flesh. No God delivered me from his fists and abominations, and none shall deliver him from his destiny on this cold, quiet night.

I entered his room and gazed upon his sleeping body. There he lay, not a clue in the world that his firstborn son would usher him into the next existence.

The moment had arrived. I was ready to taste the revenge I had sought for over 12 years. I was ready to taste his blood upon my lips and watch him transition to the afterlife. I pulled the fire poker from the backpack that rested on my shoulders. The anguish from a decade now rested in my left hand. I took one final deep breath, and in an almighty blow, the fire poker struck its target without remorse.

He lay there shivering, almost in a seizure-like state. Once he stopped convulsing, I checked his vitals to see if he was still alive. He was. I rolled him to the edge of the bed and onto the La-Z-Boy recliner. I heavily taped his hands and feet to ensure he couldn't escape my grasp once he regained consciousness.

After about three minutes, he opened his eyes. Confusion and astonishment overcame his face. I chuckled sarcastically and let his face feel the palm of my hand to ensure he had his wits about himself. At that moment, I thought I would have a long speech for him, but I could only muster the words "As salaam alaikum, brother."

The blade of the sword now rested in my sweaty palm as I placed it to his sweaty, pulsating carotid artery. I looked upon my father one last time as his breathing rapidly increased, knowing his last few moments in this world were quickly expiring. He attempted to yell, but the tape prevented any relevant sounds from escaping his lips. He jerked his body violently to free himself from the recliner, but my tape job, again, held true. I closed my eyes, and in a swift stroke, cut his throat with a clean horizontal incision. His blood covered my hands and chest as the release of years of abuse left my body. The sensation of his dying body was better than any sex I had yet to feel and experience.

As his last breath left his body, I stood there in amazement at my work, yet curious about how the human body transitions to the next stage of life, as we know it. Minutes later, after my plan was successfully executed, I began to experience an unexpected sensation that was not accounted for in my planning process. I went over every detail of this evening with delicate precision. Yet I didn't plan for this sudden, unexpected sensation. My hands trembled in fear. I panicked, as if the police or my grandmother had caught me. But neither the police nor my grandmother were there, and my grandmother still rested peacefully in her room.

Why was I feeling this way?

What was this sensation that now coursed throughout my veins? My father is dead, but why am I not elated as I set out to be? What is happening to me? Is it my father's spirit coming back to haunt me, not even five minutes after his demise? I fell to the floor as the strength left my legs and lower body. My body was in complete rejection of the thought that now traveled over the synapse of my brain. As I lay on the floor next to my father's lifeless body, it all began to make sense. My eyes then began to fill up with tears, and my jaw clenched with the anxiety of the moment. The feeling that now raced through my mind and body was none other than guilt.

There he lay, free from the burdens of this world, and I was responsible for relieving him. How could I have been so foolish? I should have let him live, and every day he breathed, he would have had to face himself in the mirror and account for his transgressions. Now I had taken his burden from him, and it was now my Cross to carry. I was in immense and unbearable pain. It felt as if my soul was lifting from my body and traveling towards the opposite side of the heavens. At that very moment, I craved and desperately needed immediate relief from the heavy burden I had caused.

In the blink of an eye, I found myself reaching inside my backpack and grasping the pistol I had for him in my hand. As the feeling of sorrow increasingly grew, the solution became even more apparent than his death. I had to take my own life. But how had this come to pass? Why? Regardless of the answers, the barrel of the weapon now rested on my temple with deadly intentions. I breathed heavily to fight the urge of sorrow and guilt, but there was only one means to this end. Shemyaza appeared in the room, but He only looked as if I was close to completing the ultimate 'Sin'.

I asked Him for help, but He only watched, as if this was written in the laws of the universe. He was emotionless. I yelled loudly in preparation for the bullet to pierce my skull. I couldn't pull the trigger immediately as I looked at Shemyaza one last time. Finally, the trigger was cocked back in concert with the hammer and my finger rested gently upon the thin curved steel. I exhaled one last time, and almost simultaneously with the loud bang, the darkness fell upon my eyes.

In that very instant, I pulled that heavy trigger, only to awaken lying in my bed in a cold, heavy sweat. It was still March 20th. I've been sleeping for only 2 hours. But when I did awake from that sleep, I realized I had a very lucid dream. Shemyaza sat there, his old familiar smell of cigar smoke surrounding him. He softly said, "You see, there are always consequences. Did you like that feeling of hopelessness and despair? Did you enjoy the feeling of guilt? Was the feeling of taking his life better than the taking of your own?"

On that early March evening, I started the process of forgiveness. Not the forgiveness for my father, but forgiving myself of the feeling that had haunted me all those years. I was yet again reborn through the refreshing of my mind and spirit. My personal Savior had shown me yet another path to freedom and salvation. I lay back down on my bed as I listened to my youngest siblings play in the hallway of our home. They sounded happy, yet completely oblivious to the plan I had contemplated only 48 hours ago.

As Shemyaza's sweet cigar smoke filled my nostrils yet again, a new plan for freedom entered my heart, mind, and spirit that cool, crisp March evening. Exodus.

CHAPTER ELEVEN

Exodus

That evening, after my vivid dream, I lay in bed contemplating the revelations that had been offered to me. My anger and lust for revenge would only add up to an unbearable feeling of despair and guilt. A guilt that would lead me to take my own life. Suicide had become an option, but I was always too afraid to do it. Somehow, I felt that even though God hadn't talked to me in years, He would not forgive me for taking the very life He had given.

After that revelation of my future, I knew there must be a different ending to my life. That nightmare was not going to define my future. I was going to be the author of an ending that was to be written in the most positive ways I could only imagine. Lying in my bed quietly, eyes closed, and tears in my eyes yet again. The familiar scent of that cigar was in my room; I didn't even have to open my eyes to acknowledge Shemyaza's presence, for I knew He was there. Sitting quietly on the edge of my bed, listening, and ever so intently, there to observe and guide my thoughts.

Even though I hadn't killed my father, the feeling was still in my heart as if I had—that feeling of betrayal. I felt dirty and ashamed. A stench reeked about my mind and spirit that was the smell of death a thousand times over.

I lay there and thought to myself, was this the feeling of disgust my sister felt when my father repeatedly raped her. Was this the guilty feeling that lived within my mother when she failed to act? A failure to act and protect her children from all danger. These feelings were harbored in my mind and physically weighed me down. Shemyaza then spoke to me after drawing from his cigar once more. There is a solution to your problems, and you already know what to do, my son. I was puzzled by his statement at first, but then a new revelation was revealed by Shemyaza. This new revelation I envisioned was freedom.

Almost a year had passed since my sister gave birth and put her child up for adoption. During that time, my mother and father permanently split, and she filed for divorce. He left the family to live with his mother. He never returned. After they split, my mother found a new sense of freedom. She would often leave home for days at a time, leaving us to fend for ourselves. My mother started traveling, wearing better clothes, dating a new boyfriend, and doing everything else that would make her happy. She went through a much-deserved reclamation process, but on the other hand, we deserved to have a mother at home. After my father left, things would get better, but the voids of loneliness and hopelessness only grew after my mother would eventually desert us, too.

Soon after the emotional disappearance and physical abandonment by my mother and father, I started to experiment with selling drugs. My siblings and I had experienced drug transactions inside our home throughout my younger years. My mother and father had no issue with smoking marijuana in front of us at any point in time. Along with smoking weed, they also had a nice-sized clientele that bought the marijuana that they grew. I was very familiar with their growing spots in the woods as well as the plants that were stashed in the attic. I witnessed them harvesting and even drying out the plants in the oven in preparation for sales.

"You better make sure that the money is correct before you give the bags out," my mother exclaimed to my sister. My oldest sister was the liaison between them and their clients. Her room window was close enough to the ground and allowed easy access for money and drug exchanges. I look back at it and see now that they had always been protected; the way the operation was set up, that the money and drugs never touched their hands. If they were ever arrested, they wouldn't have any charges except possession of illicit substances and maybe intent to distribute. From my perspective as a young man, it was ok to sell drugs to make ends meet.

During that period of the early 90s, crack cocaine reigned supreme, the king of the streets, and plenty of money was being made. If you weren't smoking crack, you were smoking weed, or even both. I learned very quickly by managing the drug money about investing and re-upping. I automatically figured out that to be successful selling at dope, you had to remain as anonymous and inconspicuous as possible. Most of the dealers became entangled with big chains and flashy cars, complete with rims and high-end sound systems. They drew attention to themselves with all the shiny shit. As expected, the shinier and flashier guys were, the more likely they were to get locked up. I remained low-key with my movements and dealings, even though I didn't make as much money as the other dealers.

Selling crack was relatively easy; if your product was good, the crackheads found you. They would even show up at your house at all hours of the night looking for a fix. That was a serious issue for me, and it was an error of judgment. I shouldn't have had junkies coming to the house especially when we were there most times by ourselves… but my drive for money superseded common sense and the need for safety.

Needless to say, my glory as a drug dealer was short-lived. My reign of selling crack lasted only for seven months, but this brief period was more than enough for my emotional state to take. Two instances led to my short run as the Nino Brown of small-town Alabama. First, there was Annette. Annette lives about two miles from me. She was a great long-standing customer who always guaranteed me at least three to four hundred dollars per month from her welfare check. One deliberate pet peeve I've always had was doing my dealings in the yard. I vowed never to do business inside someone's home. This was because almost 100 percent of my customers had children in the house; I was strongly against letting the kids see drugs because I had seen them in my home way too much.

Annette adhered to my policy and, for the most part, never asked me to sell her my products inside the house. Annette always had her five children at home, as only her oldest daughter was school age. As I watched her crack habit dramatically progress over the months, she slowly attempted to relax my standards of not conducting business in front of her kids.

One afternoon, Annette sent word for me to bring her the daily fix via homeboy, who lived across the street from her. As I approached her trailer, I didn't notice Annette sitting on her porch as she usually would. The hairs on my arm are now standing up straighter than an arrow, as my paranoia rapidly sets in. Was she setting me up? I quickly looked around to see if I noticed any unmarked police cars that were waiting for the transaction to take place. To my comfort, I didn't see any, so I had my buddy sound the horn to see if she would come to the porch. After the third horn blow, she came out to the steps and waved her hand rapidly as if to motion me to enter the house. At this point, I became increasingly skeptical of what was happening.

I borrowed a Ruger 9mm handgun from my friend just in case it was a set up move to rob me for my shit. I put one in the chamber, tucked it in my jeans, and approached the door cautiously. I knocked three times, and she came to the door half-dressed. As I walked through the door, I noticed that her trailer was oddly absent of the noise her kids usually made. Her trailer looked to be somewhat clean compared to most other junkies' homes I had seen.

After a brief exchange of pleasantries, she bluntly exclaimed to me that she was short on cash by one hundred dollars for the amount of crack she wanted. However, on this day, Annette offered me a deal to compensate for her financial constraints. I asked, "Well, what are you offering?" In my mind, I was anticipating a gold ring, jewelry, or some other form of electronics to make up the money she was short. This day would not turn out to be as simple as a material trade as I often bargained.

Let's see what you got, Annette, I said sarcastically. "Come on out, baby, she demanded."

When I looked up and saw who she called from the back room, I felt

like my heart dropped out of my chest. My eyes filled with tears, but I didn't allow them to hit my face at all. This fucking junkie had offered me to have my way her daughter in exchange for drugs. Her daughter, in all her innocence, was no more than 13 years old. What was wrong with her? There her daughter stood, scared, but willing to please her mother at all costs. I was both furious and saddened by the offer presented to me. I quickly gathered the crack I was cutting up for her, and left her house with sadness in my heart in the fastest manner that I could.

I'm sure I was not the first or the last Annette made this offer to. I was sick to my stomach. How could a mother pimp out her daughter for a twenty-minute high? How could a mother allow her daughter's self-respect, self-esteem, and dignity to be blown up in the smoke from a crack pipe? How could this drug be so debilitating to one's thought process that nothing matters except the high that they want to achieve?

Once I got to the car, I gave the gun, the crack, and the money to my homeboy. He sat there in shock, staring at the ghastly look on my face.

"You good nigga?", he asked. I assumed he was wondering what the fuck happened to me in Annette's house. I managed to nod in affirmation. I never spoke of those events to him, but I did make him promise to never sell to her under any circumstances. I never mentioned that offer to anyone in my life. That day was the last that I laid my eyes and hands on crack cocaine, or even contemplated doing anything illegal for the benefit of monetary gains. The risk of jail was too significant, but even greater was the burden that I would have to carry on my shoulders – the burden of destroying families.

After my brief stint selling crack, leaving Alabama was the only thing that I wanted to do. I knew it would take a plan as well as sacrifice to do so. I witnessed far too many people from my hometown sit in mediocrity. Generation after generation sat there in that small town in Alabama and watched their lives silently blow away with the swift breezes from the Gulf of Mexico. I couldn't accept that fate for myself.

I decided, then, that I must become my benefactor.

I decided to quit high school at the age of 18, at the end of my senior year, and take the GED test. My grades were so poor that I knew I wouldn't graduate on time. There was to be no graduation for me, not with a 1.79 GPA. I started to work with the intention of saving enough money to purchase a plane ticket and fly out to California. I revered California from what I saw on TV shows like Baywatch and The Fresh Prince of Bel Air. The beaches look so big and beautiful. We didn't have the best television in my home, but I could still tell California looked fun. As great as it sounded, Shemyaza had a way of bringing me back down to earth and keeping things in perspective. He asked what I would do about housing, food, and work when I arrived. He completely shut down my grandiose dreams of walking on the beach and enjoying the warm California sun. After discussing it with Shemyaza, I ultimately realized that California wasn't a realistic goal at that time. Shemyaza, my Savior, had a different plan for me. A plan that was unknown to me, a plan that would change the very course of my history and destiny.

CHAPTER TWELVE

Ascending the Winding Staircase

I continued to work at the Cooking Good chicken plant for seven months. I saved money and purchased my first car with a down payment of 500 dollars. I was happy with my accomplishment of saving the money, but this wasn't my plan. I wanted out of Alabama badly. The desire to leave Alabama was so great that I would lie awake at night just wanting to drive and not stop till I was far away. However, I was without the necessary resources and provisions to make such a transition. Cooking Good was tiring and demoralizing, but it was better than selling dope to my community. I worked hard to have a feeling of self-worth and accomplishment. The "live-hanging" department at the chicken plant was the worst department of all.

My job entailed hanging about 40 chickens per minute by their feet in preparation for them to be killed. It also included the chicken shit and piss that saturated my clothing by the sunrise. I had to work the overnight shift to make the most money. By accepting the third shift, my hourly pay was increased to $7.10 an hour. That job was the worst I ever had, but it made me hungry. The longer I worked at that plant, the more I wanted out. The longer I hung those chickens, the more I planned for another life. My Sunday through Thursday schedule allowed me to get paid on Friday mornings before leaving the plant. I would typically drive to a liquor store, about 15 minutes away, to cash my check without being charged more than $20 in fees.

One particular Friday, I couldn't cash my check at my normal location due to a murder investigation right in front of the store.

After driving about 10 minutes further across town, the scent of Shemyaza's sweet cigar smoke made his presence known in my car. He appeared in the passenger seat as I sat at the traffic light waiting to turn onto the block of the check cashing store. He smiled and said, "Look, my son, your Exodus awaits you." There it was, a small bright green and yellow billboard. The color scheme reminded me of the colors of beautiful tulips, surrounded by lush green grass. It reminded me of the grass I used to lie in my special place beyond the pine trees of my home.

The billboard boldly read, Hallie Turner Alternative School. I quickly pulled into the parking lot and prepared myself to go in. The crime scene investigation had placed me on this route I usually didn't take, and I coincidentally arrived when they were just opening for the day. I entered the building still wearing my work clothes, covered in feathers and chicken droppings. Although my presentation was dirty and foul-smelling, the school's administrative assistant still kindly explained that this facility was a 'work at your own pace' format. She told me that if everything went according to plan, I could meet the requirements for their upcoming graduation ceremony in about 8 weeks. I asked her, "Do you mean graduate with a diploma and walk across the stage?"

She replied, "Yes, sir, and with a cap and gown!"

I was sold. Grinning from ear to ear, I walked out of the school doors with a new sense of purpose. I was going to graduate from high school, and I could say, "To hell with that GED."

As I exited the door, I accidentally bumped into a gentleman entering the building, causing him to spill his coffee on the ground. "I'm sorry, sir," I exclaimed. "I didn't see you." I recognized he was part of the Navy by his uniform, but I couldn't recall his rank, even though I had taken NJROTC as part of my school electives. His name tag was black and had white letters that read, Petty Officer Thompson.

"No problem, young man," he replied. "I can get another cup; it was free anyway," he chuckled. "Do you go to this school?" "What are your plans after graduation?" Do you want to see the world and get paid too?"

I was like damn brother, all these questions all at once? I figured I should respond to the latter question since it mattered to me the most. I quickly replied, "Are you fucking kidding me, hell yes! How soon can you get me out this motherfucker?"

I met with Petty Officer Thompson the week after I enrolled in Hallie Turner. Petty Officer Thompson was a tall, slender man in stature. His wrinkles around his eyes let me know he was possibly in his early 50s. He spoke intelligently about the Navy, as well as about life in general. I sat attentively and listened so intensely to his tales from the Navy. All the places he had been. All the countries he had visited. It almost seemed like he knew exactly what I needed at that point in my life. As he told his stories, I would daydream and envision myself as him, greeting all the people from every place around the world. I wanted this life so bad! I wanted out of Alabama.

He quickly brought me back to reality by explaining that my GED would not be accepted, but a high school diploma would. He promised me that after I graduated from Hallie Turner, I could leave for boot camp in a matter of a month. The first person I wanted to tell was my mother. After all we had been through as a family, I still wanted to make her proud of me.

My mother's reaction to my decision to join the Navy was not well-received. She gave me a million different reasons why I shouldn't leave home. I explained to her the benefits, but she only saw the fact that I might be sent to war and come home a shell of myself, as her brother did. Little did she know, I was already a shell of myself, and this was an attempt to reclaim my life.

The days following my announcement included constant attempts to persuade me to change my mind and not sign up for military service. The more she gave me reasons not to, the more I wanted it. Knowing that her attempts were merely distractions to divert me from my path, I worked even harder to earn my diploma at Hallie Turner. As the grade reports came in as quickly as I completed them, I was pleased with the A's and B's, along with the high praises from my instructors. I did question why I couldn't get it right the first time, but I wasn't going to dwell on my past mistakes. I wanted this Exodus as badly as I wanted God to talk to me.

Around the end of March 1995, the moment I had waited for had finally come. I received my final class grade of an A, and I was eligible to graduate on April 13th. I told my parents of the date so they could attend. The actual graduation was held on a weekday around lunch, so I knew most of my family wouldn't be able to come. All I wanted was my mother and father to be present. I wanted to prove to them that I wasn't a complete failure.

On the morning of April 13th, a small layer of cool fog lay in the atmosphere and on the ground. I rose to my feet with excitement and a sense of bliss. The sweet smell of the cigar Shemyaza smoked was present, bringing a sense of comfort to the moment. I couldn't stop smiling as I brushed my teeth and washed my face. As the hot water from the shower ran over my body, a sense of completion coursed through my veins, creating an unimaginable, exhilarating feeling. I was all dressed up in my slacks, pressed shirt, and green tie to match. I drove to the auditorium to walk across that stage.

It was just 10 months ago that I decided to drop out of school, and yet here I was. There was no stopping me today. The audience was relatively small, as expected when looking from the stage. I quickly spotted my Navy recruiter, Petty Officer Thompson, in the crowd. He showed up in his uniform to demonstrate that he, as well as the Navy, was fully supportive of my becoming the newest member of their organization. Who I didn't see in the audience was my mother and father. I patiently waited near the door for them to arrive, but as the ceremony began, I knew they weren't coming—a feeling of disappointment settled over my heart. Yesterday, my mother gave me the 300 dollars I was short for my tuition; today, I needed my mother to give me her presence. Unfortunately, just like the other times, there was no one there but me and Shemyaza.

My special Savior was always at my side, and on this distinct day, He stood in the shadows of the stage. Only his soft silhouette and the orange glow of his burning cigar were noticeable. I strolled across the stage when they called my name. I had one of the biggest smiles on my face; the only smile that could compare was the one I had when I exited my mother's womb on May 5th, 1975.

After the graduation, Petty Officer Thompson took me to the local steakhouse for lunch. At this lunch, he would reveal to me the news that would change my life forever. Petty Officer Thompson informed me that my request to ship out early had been granted and that I would be leaving in two weeks. Hearing this news made me even more elated than the stroll across the stage with my diploma in my hands! I never thought I would have such a day in my life that was filled with so much happiness and joy. As a child, I never experienced the joy of birthday parties with friends. I never experienced opening Christmas presents with my brothers and sisters. I never felt the loving embrace from my parents. I never experienced the true teachings a father gives his son, or the compassion a mother gives her child. On this day, though, through all the trials, tears, pain, and abuse, those feelings of despair were replaced with a feeling that I had never experienced a single day in my life. The feeling that now made its presence known in my mind, heart, and soul could be seen all over my face from a mile away. Hope.

The two weeks I've been granted have gone by quickly. I spent much of my time with my brothers, sisters, and grandmothers. Spending time with my siblings was the highlight of it all. I felt I was doing this for them as well as for myself. I felt someday that we would all break this cycle of abuse and poverty. I was making the first step and setting the foundation for all of us to build upon. My mother still desperately tried to get me to change my mind, but I refused; I ignored all her fearful thoughts and rationale. I was not going to succumb to the fear of the unknown, as my parents had. I was going to make the move and take a leap of faith from darkness into the light.

The morning of May 18th, I awakened in my bed, excited – this was the day I made it to the top of those winding case of stairs, and glaringly peered into the eyes of that starry Heaven above. As I cleared my throat and eyes, I noticed Shemyaza sitting on the corner of my bed as usual. Just as many days, months, and years before, He was there faithfully. "Good morning, my son!" he exclaimed.

I smiled, feeling pretty sure that He already knew what was on my mind that day. I got up with a quiet sense of anticipation, ate a quick breakfast, and carefully packed the last of my few clothes into a small black suitcase — my heart beating a little faster with every step. This was it!

My recruiter had instructed me to meet him at the Wiregrass Commons Mall by 2 p.m. I couldn't be late — not today. Not for anything. I borrowed my mother's truck and made the rounds, saying my final goodbyes to family and friends. When I arrived back home, I let my mother know I was ready to go. I placed my fully packed bag in the truck and waited patiently for her to come outside.

As I stood there, it hit me — this was the last time I'd ever set foot in that house. The house that had been the backdrop of so much pain and heartache was finally about to disappear in my rearview mirror. For good.

My mother eventually came out, started the truck, and we began the quiet drive to the mall. We didn't talk much. The only sounds in the cab were the soft hum of the engine and the wind rushing through my open window. I leaned back in the seat, closed my eyes, and let the cool May breeze wash over me.

As I sat there, I tried to picture my life twenty years from now. Where would I be? Who would I become? I could only dream of peace, of hope, of love. That's all I wanted. That's all my lonely heart ever yearned for: peace, hope, and love. I wanted better. And for the first time, I felt like I was finally on the road to finding it.

* * * * *

As we approached the mall, my mother broke the serene silence with her last pitch to keep me stuck in Alabama. I never understood why she didn't see that the city and the state had nothing to offer me at this point in my life. For me, Alabama only provided shackles and structures that have only failed me. Or maybe she did know what was to come, and she wanted to prevent it from happening for her selfish reasons. Perhaps she knew, with a clear mind and judgment, that the truth would be revealed to me. The truth that would break those generational chains of poverty, abuse, and self-hate. A truth that would cast doubt and raise questions regarding her role as a mother during my childhood.

My mother and I arrived at the mall at 1:48 p.m. On the side of the

Sears department store, I noticed him standing once again in his uniform. Petty Officer Thompson was there waiting patiently for my arrival. My mother gave me her last spiel about the military as I smiled and acknowledged her opinion. Before I left the truck, she gave me a Fossil wallet she had purchased from the mall the day before my departure. My mother begged me profusely not to go with my recruiter, tears falling from her eyes. Part of me felt guilty and unsure of the decision I was about to make, but that was only a tiny part of me. The rest of me knew what lay ahead if I stayed in Alabama. Mediocrity.

I believed deep down in my heart, through all of the trials and tribulations, that mediocrity was not part of my DNA. As I listened to the last of her pleas, I respectfully told her it was time for us to say goodbye. For me, it was a farewell to the past. Farewell to the rural Alabama community where I resided for 18 years. Farewell to the non-believers and all those who wrote me off for failure. Farewell to all those who turned their backs on me when I needed help the most. A Great Farewell to all those who rendered a promising, bright, and worthy child, who only wanted to be loved, and allowed him to be an invisible, starving little boy.

I hugged my mother with little emotion, and then wiped away the tears that had momentarily flowed. I told her it would be all right. I then softly kissed her right cheek, told her I loved her, and opened the squeaky truck door. Upon stepping on the pavement of the parking lot, my knees buckled slightly from the anticipation of this momentous occasion. My feet and toes tingled from the sensations of the moment that lay before me. I was doing it! I was finally leaving Alabama!

I placed my suitcase in the back seat, got into the Petty Officer's

Thompson's government-issued vehicle, and gently sat in the passenger seat. Without hesitation, I quickly buckled my seatbelt and leaned my chair back just to get comfortable. He asked me, "Are you sure this is what you want?"

I replied emphatically, Yes, sir!" It was with that confident confirmation on May 18, 1995, that I gave myself to the United States Navy. It was on this very day that I was headed to Chicago to begin my Navy career. It was this day that I will never forget, as it marked my independence and liberation. It was this day that was to be my Exodus from tyranny and persecution. It was this day that the Heavens shined upon me, and I opened my eyes to bear witness to the new beginnings that lay before me.

As we slowly drove off, I quickly turned to look over my left shoulder at my mother one last time. I could see her still sobbing and wiping tears away from her saddened face. I waved with my right hand out the window and smiled, knowing that this was the last time I was ever to call this small town in Alabama home. Just as Dorothy was swept up and away by that powerful summer twister in Kansas, I, too, was swept away in Petty Officer Thompson's car as well as in my own emotions that presented themselves on my face.

As I refocused my eyes from her truck to the back seat of my recruiter's car, I saw Him there ever so quietly in His presence. There He sat, so patiently and calm—my Savior. Shemyaza was the bearer of the light I needed in the midst of my darkness. He remained dressed in the same suit He had appeared in all those years back. All those years of guidance and wisdom, He provided me. All those years of mental and physical strength so that I could endure the pain and heartache from my mother and father, He provided me. All those years of survival, he helped me bury the very emotions that made me human—all those years of chaos had led me to this very moment of unfamiliarity and uncertainty. All those years of silence and unanswered prayers from God. I was now answering all those years of questions. I became my own Savior.

On this glorious day, He too was right by my side. His omnipresence provided the stability and strength I needed, just as He had done all those years before. And just as all the times he had appeared before me, the familiar sweet smell of His cigar smoke coming from the back seat of the recruiter's car let me know everything was going to be all right.

,

ACKNOWLEDGEMENTS

First and foremost, I lift my voice in thanksgiving, praise, and reverence to the Creator—the Divine Architect of the Heavens and the Earth, the unseen Presence who dwells in all things and surrounds us with grace and mystery. Without the guidance, protection, and eternal love of that Great Spirit, I would not be here today. To the One who is beyond all names, who speaks through silence and breathes through wind and memory—I offer my deepest gratitude. I also honor the sacred duality—the Divine Masculine and the Sacred Feminine—whose balanced energies give life to all creation and continue to nourish my soul. May this harmony remain in me, and in all who seek peace in this world.

I bow in honor to my ancestors—those noble spirits whose footprints I walk in, whose wisdom echoes in my bones. Though you have journeyed into the spirit world, your presence remains deeply felt in the unfolding of my life. I offer special homage to my grandmothers, ever-watchful, ever-loving—your prayers still shelter me, your love still carries me. And to my beloved kin who have transitioned: Rose Freeman and David Freeman (Big Daddy), Effie Lee Whitten, James Balkom, Catherine Balkom—thank you. Thank you for enduring, for paving the way, for gifting me with the strength of your names and the power of your legacy. I love and miss you deeply, and I carry you with me in every breath and every step.

To the Magnificent 6—my cherished brothers and sisters—this work is for you. This story, this testimony, this offering: it is ours. Bound not by blood alone, but by struggle, by shared survival, by unshakable love. Together, we shattered the generational chains of pain, and through the grace of God, we rose above the patterns into which we were born. We became different. We became better. And now, let us turn our hearts to the future. Let us build something radiant for our children. Let us be the protectors of their dreams, the guardians of their legacy. The time has come for reunion, for healing. I am ready. I long to go home—may the doors of home be open; may the embrace be waiting. I've been away too long.

To the friends who stood beside me, believed in me, and held space for me when my voice faltered—thank you. Thank you to those who encouraged me to keep writing, who reminded me of my purpose, who read my early words with love and gave truth without judgment. Your support has been both an anchor and a sail. And to every soul who has touched my life—students I taught, comrades with whom I served in the Armed Forces, colleagues who worked beside me, friends known and unknown, named and unnamed—your presence has left a mark on my journey. If I have forgotten to mention you by name, know that your impact is not forgotten. From the depths of my heart: thank you. May we continue forward with grace, wisdom, and the light of gratitude guiding our way.

AFTERWORD

As a child, my Saturday mornings were filled with the familiar ritual of watching cartoons, much like those of countless others in my generation. Amid the bright colors and exaggerated humor, a recurring motif quietly embedded itself in my awareness: the image of a character torn between a tiny angel perched on one shoulder and a devil on the other. These figures, invisible to the outside world, engaged in an internal dialogue that represented conflicting moral impulses. The angel whispered restraint, empathy, and wisdom; the devil offered indulgence, defiance, and immediate gratification. Though animated for humor, these scenes symbolized a deeper metaphysical struggle—a dramatization of the divided human will.

These childhood images planted early seeds for my later philosophical reflections. Even then, I intuited that the battle unfolding on screen was not external, but deeply internal, occurring in the hidden recesses of the mind. The characters acted based on these unseen conversations, their decisions shifting according to context and circumstance. It became clear, even in my youth, that morality was not always a fixed compass, but often a negotiation between competing inner voices. The figures of the angel and devil were crude symbols, but they mirrored something real: the tension between higher aspirations and primal impulses, between conscience and desire.

Looking back, I recognize these inner dialogues as the early architecture of my spiritual understanding. The angel and devil became representations of what many traditions have named as God and the Devil, not as external beings, but as symbolic expressions of inner forces. My conscious mind—the realm of choice, clarity, and intentionality—began to take shape through these moments. Yet, beneath that layer, the unconscious stirred with unprocessed emotions, hidden fears, and lingering pain. It was here, in the unresolved depths of my psyche, that the trauma of my early life settled, shaping how I saw the world and, more crucially, how I saw myself.

Thus, my reality was not merely a product of what I observed externally, but of what was being contested within me. The subconscious and conscious minds were not only in dialogue but in competition for authorship of my narrative. Philosophy teaches that the self is not a fixed essence but a becoming, one shaped by memory, emotion, and thought. For me, childhood trauma became both the veil and the lens through which reality was interpreted. That inner battleground, introduced through a cartoon's simplification, matured into a lifelong meditation on freedom, responsibility, and the enduring complexity of the human condition.

Permit me then to offer my perspective—one shaped not merely by intellectual inquiry, but by years of sustained contemplation, disciplined study, and earnest prayer directed toward that which many call God: the transcendent source of all being, wisdom, and awareness. This is not a conclusion hastily reached, nor a belief blindly inherited. Still, a position arrived at through the slow and often painful process of existential questioning and inner refinement. In seeking understanding, I have not only turned to sacred texts and philosophical works but also to the silent spaces within, where intuition meets reason and the soul communes with the ineffable.

My reflections are born out of a deep reverence for what some traditions refer to as the Divine Mind, the Logos, or the Absolute— terms that point not to a being among beings, but to the very ground of Being itself. In this search, I have discovered that true knowledge is not merely the accumulation of data, but a form of remembering—

a return to something already present in the depths of the soul. Thus, the insights I now share are not simply conclusions of thought, but revelations granted through grace, humility, and the gradual unveiling of the inner life before the eternal.

The Conscious Mind as Divine Presence

In the contemplative traditions of philosophy and mysticism alike, the conscious mind has often been viewed as a sacred mirror—a luminous reflection of the divine within the human soul. It is this conscious awareness that enables us to perceive ourselves, to question, to discern, and to make choices. Just as the divine is described in many traditions as the Logos, or the ordering principle of the cosmos, so too does the conscious mind bring order to experience and provide direction for action. Through it, the human being becomes a vessel of volition, capable of transcending mere instinct and participating in the unfolding of higher moral and spiritual truths.

The Creative Power of Awareness

To be conscious is not only to witness reality but to shape it. From this perspective, the conscious mind is the locus of co-creation—it is the divine artist within, forming meaning out of chaos, beauty out of potential. Through attention, intention, and will, we give form to the formless, much as the divine breath was said to animate the void. Ethical action, creative endeavor, and spiritual practice all originate in this sacred center. When aligned with values such as love, wisdom, and compassion, the conscious mind becomes not merely an observer of life, but a participant in divine unfolding—what some might call the imago Dei, the image of God in us.

The Unconscious as the Shadowed Depth

If the conscious mind symbolizes divine light, then the unconscious—what Carl Jung termed the "shadow"—can be seen as the realm of forgotten gods and exiled truths. It is the dark mirror, the place where denied desires, repressed fears, and unresolved wounds reside. Spiritually, this domain has often been symbolized as the adversary—the devil, the tempter, or the trickster. However, in a more nuanced interpretation, these symbols do not refer to external forces of evil, but to the interior dimensions of the self that remain unseen and therefore remain unintegrated. The unconscious is not evil per se; rather, it is dangerous only in proportion to our ignorance of it.

The Burden of the Unseen

When ignored or misunderstood, the contents of the unconscious may manifest in distorted forms, including irrational behavior, destructive impulses, and compulsive patterns. Like unacknowledged truths, they find expression in dreams, projections, emotional outbursts, or inner conflict. From a philosophical perspective, these disruptions are not signs of moral failure but rather invitations to deeper self-awareness. Spiritually, they may represent the soul's cry for wholeness. The archetype of the devil, then, serves less as a moral condemnation and more as a mythic symbol of the internal chaos that arises when the psyche is divided against itself.

Integration as Spiritual Alchemy

The true spiritual task is not to banish the shadow, but to integrate it. This is the path of inner alchemy: to transmute the lead of unconscious drives into the gold of conscious insight. In this light, salvation is not escape from the self, but reconciliation within the self. The conscious mind must become not a tyrant over the unconscious, but a compassionate steward—illumining, understanding, and ultimately redeeming the darker aspects of the psyche. It is through this integration that the human being moves toward individuation, or in spiritual terms, toward union with the divine.

The Unity of Opposites

Ultimately, the dichotomy between the conscious and unconscious, God and the devil, light and shadow, is not absolute but dialectical. Each depends on the other to reveal the fullness of the human condition. The conscious mind offers order and clarity, the unconscious, depth and vitality. When these polarities are harmonized, the individual awakens to a deeper dimension of being—a state in which divinity is not found in purity alone, but in the embrace of wholeness. Thus, the divine spark within us does not extinguish the shadow but illuminates it, transforming darkness into wisdom and division into sacred unity.

Verily, the question of who or what is God is not answered in the tongues of men alone, nor the wisdom of the world, but is revealed in the sacred journey of the soul. It is written, "The kingdom of God is within you" (Luke 17:21), and so it is through self-examination, through the refining fire of affliction, and through the whisper of the Spirit that the knowledge of the Most High is made known. For me, it was in the valley of sorrow, in the wilderness of my youth, amid the shadows of pain and childhood trauma, that the Lord met me. There, He lifted the veil from my eyes, and I beheld not only His mercy but the beginning of my redemption.

Praise be to God, for in His light I found healing, and in His truth, I found liberty. The burden of my past, once too heavy for me to bear, was laid at the foot of the cross, where Christ Himself bore my iniquities and carried my griefs. What once bound me in chains has now become a testimony of freedom, and what once brought shame now bears witness to the power of divine grace. "For whom the Son sets free, is free indeed" (John 8:36). My salvation—full and everlasting—has not come through my strength, nor by any merit of my own, but by the lovingkindness of God and the holy words and teachings of Jesus Christ, the Lamb of God and the Light of the world.

By His mercy, I have not only overcome the trials and tribulations set before me, but have been called to be a vessel—a servant in His field, a light unto those still walking through darkness. For many, some suffer in silence, whose inner battles rage unseen, whose wounds run deep. To those like these, I say: You are not forsaken. The Lord thy God is near to the brokenhearted and saves those crushed in spirit (Psalm 34:18). He knows your sorrow, hears your cries, and walks beside you even when you do not see Him. Call upon His name, for "everyone who calls upon the name of the Lord shall be saved" (Romans 10:13).

If these words find you still in battle—fighting the devils within, wrestling with despair or doubt—know this: God has not abandoned you. Even now, He is calling, patiently waiting for your heart to turn toward Him. Trust in His guidance, lean not on your understanding, and listen for His voice, for He is gentle, and His yoke is easy. I am humbled beyond measure to be counted among the redeemed, and I declare with all my heart: To God be the glory, forever and ever! Amen.

www.ingramcontent.com/pod-product-compliance
Lightning Source LLC
Chambersburg PA
CBHW031222120626
46545CB00003B/947